THE
FUNERAL

-◄{ VESTIGE }►-
OR VALUE?

THE
FUNERAL
--⊰{ VESTIGE }⊱--
OR VALUE?

PAUL E. IRION

ABINGDON PRESS / NASHVILLE / NEW YORK

THE FUNERAL: VESTIGE OR VALUE?

Copyright © 1966 by Abingdon Press

Library of Congress Catalog Card Number: 66-11451

Scripture quotations unless otherwise noted are
from the Revised Standard Version of the Bible,
copyrighted 1946 and 1952 by the Division of
Christian Education, National Council of
Churches, and are used by permission.

SET UP, PRINTED, AND BOUND BY THE
PARTHENON PRESS, AT NASHVILLE,
TENNESSEE, UNITED STATES OF AMERICA

DEDICATED TO

Mary Jean Irion

"She opens her mouth with wisdom,
and the teaching of kindness is
on her tongue."—Prov. 31:26

PREFACE

Possibly not since the medieval emphasis on the art of dying has there been such widespread popular concern for the funeral. Best-selling satires, feature stories in magazines, articles in journals of the social sciences, television documentaries, and congressional hearings have focused the attention of the nation upon this event which normally in our culture accompanies death.

There have been numerous voices raised to claim that the funeral no longer has meaning for our time. It is seen as a vestige of past eras, an anachronism, a wasteful, unneeded, empty ceremony that outlived its usefulness long ago. These critics have complained that commercial interests and religious institutions have sought to keep the shell of the funeral alive out of selfish interest or misguided dedication to the status quo. At the same time it must be admitted that there are some who, more or less admitting their vested interest, have stubbornly insisted that the funeral be preserved intact without question.

It remains for the serious student of the funeral to ask the question: Is the funeral vestige or value? The answer to this query is not simple. With good reason the contemporary funeral is confronted with ambivalence. There is much to be dissatisfied with in its present form. And yet, there is apparent in the proper construction of its meanings and functions much that is of value. There is too much of value in it

7

to encourage one to accede to the suggestions that the funeral be summarily discarded as an expensive and meaningless luxury.

This study sets out to seek to isolate and describe the valuable functions of the funeral. It will evaluate the contemporary funeral in the light of these functions and will propose new designs which conserve the valuable functions of the funeral, investing them where necessary in new forms.

My concern for the funeral is not new. A decade ago I sought to relate modern psychological insights into the dynamics of bereavement to the funeral service. This concern has not waned. It is stimulated by the deepening of the meaningful relationship between theology and the behavioral sciences. It has profited from the emphasis of Seward Hiltner and others on the development of pastoral theology as the product of the minister's theological reflection upon his pastoral operations. It is shaped by a revival of liturgical worship which emphasizes the necessity for the participation of all the people of God in the service of worship. It is stirred by the current debate regarding the structure of the church and its ministry in parochial versus nonparochial forms. It is moved by the far-reaching critiques of the funeral which have advanced on numerous fronts in the past several years. All of these influences converge to turn me to probe the funeral for its meaning and mission.

One of the wholesome things about the contemporary attention given to the funeral is that it has caused many individuals to do some serious and evaluative thinking about a custom which has been taken very much for granted. It is my hope that this book will serve as a vital aid in such assessment of the funeral. No effort has been made here to work out every answer in detail. The major purpose of this study is to offer a basis for investigation, questioning, criticism, and reconstruction of the funeral.

It is hoped that this study will form the basis for positive discussion of the function and forms of the funeral by all those who are concerned. Groups within local churches, members of memorial societies, and informal discussion groups will profit from an objective, serious, personal probing of the meanings of the funeral founded upon data from theology and the sciences of man. An appendix (pp. 225-30) contains a suggested discussion guide for such a group consideration of the funeral.

Questions need to be asked and answered about why people plan the type of funerals that they do. Attention needs to be given to a variety of criteria for judging the effectiveness and value of the funeral and its alternatives. Correctives need to be developed for evaluations of the funeral based solely on economic considerations or upon neurotic efforts to escape the reality of death and bereavement. Thorough, thoughtful encounter with the meaning of the funeral is the only way in which it can be seen as a value rather than a vestige.

PAUL E. IRION

CONTENTS

1

Picture of a
Funeral

Any serious consideration of the funeral must
have as its basis some kind of picture of the practices which
are most commonly followed in our society. Such a picture
would be helpful in two ways. First of all, it would tend to
avoid the difficulties which arise when one begins to generalize
on the basis of too limited experience. It is all too easy to
follow the reasoning of the chap who reported, "All Indians
walk single file. At least the one I saw did." Any adequate picture of the funeral has to be a composite, fitting together a
number of perspectives and angles of experience.

Secondly, the focus from which such a picture is produced
has to be sufficiently broad to include the majority of significant variables. A color picture is more descriptive than a picture which has only black and white as its variables. In order
to improve the accuracy of a picture of the contemporary
funeral, a considerable number of variables have to be taken
into account. Some effort needs to be made to examine
regional differences, including not only sections of our nation
but also the differences which grow out of urban, suburban,
or rural orientations. Ethnic differences must be taken into
account, recognizing that traditions of various national and
racial groups influence some American funeral practices. Economic and social differences, levels of the standard of living,
types of self-employment, or employment by others affect the
picture. Since the vast majority of funerals involve participation by a minister there will be a reflection of a denominational

stance as well as the personal predilection of the particular pastor who takes part. Finally, there are the variations that are produced by the considered thought or whim of the individuals and families most centrally involved in a particular funeral.

With so many variables we find ourselves in somewhat the same situation as a photographer who attempts to take a family portrait of a fairly sizable clan. Almost invariably someone will move or close his eyes at the crucial moment. In direct proportion to the size of the group one has to relax his expectation of perfection in the picture. If one wants a clear picture of Grandma and Grandpa, one may have to settle for a slightly blurred Cousin Mary or little Johnnie.

In an effort to get an impression of the appearance of the contemporary American funeral a questionnaire was sent to 160 ministers, representing ten major Protestant denominations in both city and town settings in eight major geographical regions in the United States. They were asked to answer a number of questions about the funerals which they personally conducted in the last year. These reports described more than two thousand funerals. The purpose of this survey was not to establish statistical trends but to get some representative basis for describing the state of the funeral in present-day America.

The Pattern

A rather general pattern is followed when a death occurs. Often the first step is the calling of a funeral director who removes the body of the deceased to his establishment. Families which have a meaningful relationship to a church will notify the pastor of the death. As soon as is convenient, members of the family will meet with the funeral director to make the arrangements for the funeral. In the case of families without strong church connections it is usually at this point that a minister is contacted and requested to conduct the funeral. Sometimes this request is made through the funeral home rather than the family of the deceased. Following preparation of the body, the family may privately see the body in the casket which they have selected. Then in most communities there are stated hours for public visitation at the funeral home where the body may be viewed. Friends and relatives will call at hours when members of the family are present to receive their condolences. In some communities only a few hours are set aside for such visitation, in others representatives of the family are at the funeral home during the afternoon and evening hours of the days before the funeral. In most communities the funeral is held on the afternoon of the third day following the death. In some sections of the country, particularly in the South, the interval between the time of death and the funeral is shorter. Following the funeral service, which is conducted either in the funeral home or in the church of the deceased, there is a procession of close friends and relatives of the family by automobile to the place of interment. There a brief committal service is held. In some communities, especially those with a small-town orientation, a supper may be served by neighbors and friends for the bereaved family before they return to their homes.

There seems to be general agreement that in most communities the place of the funeral is shifting from the church to the funeral home. Of the more than two thousand funerals reported in the questionnaires referred to above, less than one third were conducted in the church. In the urban areas this proportion went much lower, while in decidedly town and country sections there was still a rather general use of church facilities. It was also noted from the questionnaires that in certain instances pastors, particularly in the Episcopal and Lutheran churches, were reversing the trend by education programs and by establishment of parish policies strongly recommending funerals in the church. Even with regional and parochial exceptions a ratio of three to one holds true for the number of services in the mortuary and those in church.

An effort was made in the questionnaire to get a composite view of the various elements which make up the present-day funeral: music, scripture readings, prayers, sermons.

Some sort of music was used in the vast majority of funeral services. In many instances this was limited to instrumental music, either organ or recording. Provision for such music is made in most funeral homes. Vocal music provided by a soloist or small choral ensemble was reported by less than half of the pastors. It would also appear that vocal music was considerably less commonly a part of the funeral in urban areas than in town and country sections. The singing of a congregational hymn was much less common. It was reported by about one fifth of the ministers. It would probably be found only in services which were conducted in the church, which accounts in part for the rarity of this practice.

When pastors in the survey were asked to indicate the theme of scriptural passages which they used in funeral services, there was rather broad agreement on four themes. They are: the Christian hope for resurrection, the sustaining power of God, the Christian understanding of death, and the Christian understanding of life. Much less emphasis was given to themes like the frailty of life and the will of God.

Similar information was sought regarding the theme of prayers which appear most commonly in orders for the burial of the dead. It was found that almost all of the pastors surveyed offered prayers centered around intercession for the mourners in their need and thanksgiving for the providence of God. Much less often were prayers of submission to the will of God offered. Half of the pastors indicated that the Lord's Prayer was prayed in unison by those attending.

It is sometimes assumed that the funeral sermon is no longer commonly a part of the service. Among the pastors surveyed, however, four out of every five indicate that they customarily deliver a brief sermon or address in the funeral. The most commonly cited themes for these sermons were:

efforts to meet the personal needs of the mourners, conveying the comfort of the Christian faith, and interpreting the Christian understanding of death. Considerably less attention was given to the themes of bearing witness to the values of Christian living and interpreting the will of God in the context of the situation. About two fifths of the pastors made personal references to the deceased in their sermons. About a fourth of the pastors customarily read a factual obituary, while only a very small number used a eulogy in the service.

The majority of the pastors surveyed indicated that the funerals they conducted were fifteen to thirty minutes in length. Only rarely were there reports of services which lasted less than fifteen minutes. Occasionally pastors reported services which lasted more than thirty minutes. The customary committal service is not included in these time reports.

An effort was made in the survey to seek reactions and reports on features which are commonly regarded as trends in American funeral practice. The pastors were asked to comment on their observation of changing attendance patterns, cremations, and memorial services.

Although there are probably some regional variations, there seems to be a growing observance of viewing or visitation hours when friends and relatives call at the mortuary to view the body of the deceased and to offer their sympathy to the immediate family of mourners. Pastors indicate they observe that fewer people are attending funerals than did in the past. It is also indicated that attendance is usually larger at a church funeral than one in the funeral home. This may be due to the fact that church funerals are planned for persons who are well known or where large attendance is anticipated.

Ministers surveyed were asked to report how many burials and how many cremations followed their funeral services during the past year. Of the total number of funerals and memorial services reported, 6.5 percent employed cremation for the disposition of the body. Considerable regional variation was noted. Cremation is more common in areas which are more urban in their orientation. It was interesting to note that when ministers were asked to describe plans for their own funerals, 17 percent of those surveyed indicated that they preferred to be cremated.

A third trend which was touched by the survey is the practice of holding a memorial service in lieu of a funeral. Only a very small number, less than 2 percent, of the services reported were of this nature. There was no particular regional variation apparent on this subject. Again, however, it was observed that 28 percent of the pastors surveyed would prefer a memorial service for themselves.

Such is the picture of present-day funeral practices which we have taken. On the basis of this description there are several problem areas which begin to appear in our consideration of the contemporary funeral.

Emerging Problems

One problem involves the relationship of time to participation. In a very real sense, as we shall demonstrate later, the funeral is social in nature. Part of its value and validity rests upon the degree to which a community that is meaningful to the mourners participates in the ritual. It appears that one of the major shifts in funeral practice in recent times is the custom of paying respect to the deceased and conveying sympathy to the bereaved by going to the mortuary for the visitation or viewing, rather than by attending the funeral service. A sizable number of pastors commented on this changing pattern. Most of them suggested that work schedules were the major causes for the new form.

This changing pattern of limited participation in the funeral service means that the funeral focuses primarily on the family rather than on the larger community. Although some of the critiques of the funeral would regard this as a proper thing, the observations of anthropology and social psychology described in a later chapter indicate that the larger social dimension is integral to the function of the funeral.

Some of the observations made on the basis of the survey bear out the trend for the funeral to become more private than public. Note the way in which corporate aspects are lacking in so many of the services. Congregational hymns are not commonly sung. The Lord's Prayer in unison, perhaps the simplest and most acceptable form of corporate participation, is reported to be a part of the funeral by only half of the ministers surveyed. It would appear that most often the funeral is a monologue of the pastor directed toward the bereaved family while any others, if there be such, are passive onlookers.

Yet another problem indicated by this brief overview of the funeral is that ministers are regularly called upon to conduct funeral services for families who are unrelated to the church. The pastor is then faced with the choice of leading a burial service which may be meaningless or irrelevant to the mourners or of reducing the service to sentimental generalities and pious clichés. Part of this difficulty is lack of adequate definition of the funeral. Is it a religious service, a cultural ritual, or both? Is it worship, superstition, custom, therapy? Only when one has been able to probe the definition of the funeral can one begin to assess its function.

That there is widespread dissatisfaction with the modern funeral is unquestionable. The discontentment of some is due to their conviction that ancient forms and rituals for marking death are no longer meaningful in the present era. Others are dissatisfied with the contemporary funeral because they believe that it has been reshaped from its earlier purposes by the inadequate views of life and death held by modern man.

In our attempt to undergird the values which can be found in the funeral we must examine carefully both of these sources of disenchantment with the funeral.

2

Death and Contemporary
American Man

The Freudian dictum that all behavior has meaning is equally applicable to individuals and societies. The way in which a social group meets the death of one of its members is not merely random behavior. There is a rationale which guides the development of the rituals and ceremonies observed by a group in this crisis event. These rites convey the significant values of the culture and also, probably in a somewhat lesser degree, influence the development of values within the culture. There is a real connection between a way of dying and a way of life.

Ruth Benedict, in her classical study *Patterns of Culture,*[1] provides a number of illustrations of that interaction between the major matrix of a cultural pattern and the funeral practices of a people. The general tone of the culture, the Dionysian or Apollonian mode, affects a people's view of death and guides their ritualistic concretizing of this view. The way in which death is met and dealt with, just as the way of life, is a representation of the prevailing values of a people.

Every group, from the most primitive to the most sophisticated, seeks to develop some kind of wholistic understanding of human existence. Each major event of life is placed within a context that encompasses as much as possible of human experience. Only in this way can some meaning be found in the

[1] Ruth Benedict, *Patterns of Culture* (New York: The New American Library, 1959).

20

routine and the extraordinary events of the individual life. As we have already pointed out, some of this meaning is conveyed in rituals through which a single event, such as the death of an individual, is placed into the context of the total understanding of life and death.

Our investigations can proceed in logical sequence from a study of the prevailing values found in the modern American view of life, the influence of these values on the understanding of death, and the effect upon the funeral of the meanings with which life and death are invested.

The Past

Although I do not intend to present a lengthy historical survey of views of life and death in past generations, it must be acknowledged that a marked contrast exists between past and present views.

Early America was influenced in sizable measure by the prevailing views of life and death in the Western world. The Puritanism of the colonial period exercised formative influence on a great deal of later American political, social, economic, intellectual, and religious life. The Calvinistic roots of the Puritan view saw life as a preparation for death. This was not a repetition of the morbidity of the medieval preoccupation with death, as seen in the characteristic art and literature of that period, the *Totentanz*, an allegorical art form showing Death leading off his victims in a ghastly dance, and books on the art of dying. Nevertheless, life was seen in seventeenth- through nineteenth-century America as moving toward the climactic experience of death. Confrontation with the reality of death maintained a tone of seriousness and earnestness in life. Work, meaning, fulfillment were understood not only in relationship to life but in relationship to death as well.

The major characteristic of this point of view was that life and death were regarded as related, joined on a continuum.

To be sure, the unique aspects of each were acknowledged, but they were seen as coming together in human experience. Meaning flowed freely between the two realms. People did not necessarily become morbidly obsessed with thoughts of dying nor desiring death, and there was honest recognition and confrontation of death as present reality. Life and death were not held apart.

This point of view was called into question by the spreading influence of the Enlightenment and its heirs. The deism of the eighteenth century, the increasing dimensions of humanism, the world view of modern science had two major effects. They established a breach in the continuum of life and death, separating the two, and they invested the realm of life solely with meaning. Death no longer possessed any meaning; therefore, it could not contribute any meaning to life. It was fundamentally irrelevant to living.

Franz Borkenau has developed the thesis that cultures can be characterized as death-defying, death-accepting, and death-denying.[2] Borkenau sees our American culture in a period of transition from a death-defying to a death-denying stance. In the past the Christian understanding of new life after death made it possible for man to face death defiantly because he saw the possibility of the overcoming of the ultimate power of death to destroy. He did not need to separate life from death because he could confront death as reality.

However, loss of this conviction in the possibility of resurrection requires man to take a new stance. In our age, as described by Borkenau, man struggles to deny death. He possesses no basis for defiance because he can have no more than an illusory control over death. Death is an ever-present threat, but man cannot admit it to himself. His own personal resources, his very selfhood, are not sufficiently grounded in reality to enable him to accept death with equanimity. So

[2] Franz Borkenau, "The Concept of Death," *The Twentieth Century*, April, 1955, pp. 313-29.

denial is the course left open to him. We see, then, that the pattern of denial requires a radical separation of death from life. If such a divorce is not accomplished, the pattern of denial must also encompass life. In fact, my position in this book is that denial of the reality of death does result in diminution of the meaning and the reality of life.

The Present

The advancing frontier on the North American continent and the accompanying rapid extension of the horizons of political, economic, and social life have played their parts in the emergence of a new understanding of death. This process continues as a dynamic force in American life and thought today. Basically, the process is this: as life and death are separated radically in man's reflection on human experience, more and more attention is given to life. Thus we have to approach the present American understanding of death through an understanding of American life.

Let us turn to the present American scene to examine and evaluate the elements in the view of life which are determinative of the view of death.

It is not my intention here to seek to describe discrete individual experiences. This would be a practical impossibility. And yet, we can talk about the general ethos or tone of our culture which in one way or another affects every person. Certainly there are individual exceptions. But on the whole there is a valid general impression we can receive from observing the American scene. If we were to do no more than examine the output of the media of mass communication, we would be able to point to a feeling tone that is regarded as normative even in the face of numerous individual exceptions. For example, the current status of the national economy is one of high productivity and prosperity. It might be argued that this prosperity has no meaning for the unemployed man who was automated from his job. As an individual he may not be prosperous, and still his life is touched by national prosperity whether it be in terms of new job opportunities, or retraining projects, or War on Poverty programs. It is legitimate, then, to speak of a broad cultural tone even though substantial exceptions can be noted.

There are a number of components in the contemporary American way of life to which we must give attention.

Expansionism

There is a dynamic quality in our culture which was denoted in the writings of Frederick Jackson Turner as the frontier spirit. One of the paradigms of American living is the expansionism of this spirit. For more than two centuries the context of living was a land of unlimited horizons within the realm of possible attainment. Life was turning outward into areas of available opportunity. Just as land areas were wrested from the wilderness, so expansionism came to imply the consolidation and control of vast areas of living. Repeatedly the pattern was: exploration, colonization, organization. The prospering of the nation through industrialization, education, commerce, and science gave man increasing control of life as more and more of it came within his expanding horizons.

This expansive spirit is still seen in contemporary life even though automated factories have replaced the farm homestead and computers do the work of clerks. Industrialization and the development of corporate business have recast much of the old individualism of the frontier. At the same time they have done little to blunt its expansionism, directing it to broadening consumer markets and increasing productivity. Or we might say that the present explosion of scientific knowledge symbolized in the space age represents a recapitulation of the frontier experience. Instead of finding trails to rich valleys beyond the mountains, man is exploring possible pathways to the planets. So rapidly are horizons expanding that the feeling tone of the day is one of expectation: we assume that it is just a matter of time until obstacles can be overcome.

Even though it may not be true of every single individual, on the ordinary, everyday level of life this same kind of disposition pertains. For a sizable segment of the society, particularly in the middle class, there is an expanding way of life, higher standard of living, upward social mobility, and rising educational level. The desire to expand has become one of the major drives of this culture.

We should not assume that expansionism is limited to middle-class culture. While it is true that other elements of our population are limited by circumstances and cannot easily break out of their boundaries, the aspiration for expansion is easily awakened in them. This can be seen, for example, in the struggle for freedom and equality of the American Negro in this decade. Too long his horizons have been extremely constricted by gross discrimination, inferior education, substandard housing, menial employment. The thrusts of the Freedom Revolution now indicate that, at least in his aspirations, the pattern of expansionism is seen. However, thoughtful reflection on this expansive struggle for freedom and equality would cause one to hope that such aspirations will not be restricted by the superficiality that has too often characterized the expansionism of the middle class with its status seeking and sensate culture.

Even though our contemporary culture gives evidence of growing estrangement from so-called middle-class values, expansionism does not appear to be among those elements being abandoned. The direction of expansion may be changed, but the phenomenon itself remains. While some will seek to expand their possessions or their influence, others will work toward an expansion of their knowledge. Still others may strive for the expansion of their freedom. Some may have profound goals, while others seek only the most superficial aims. But all are living basically in the mode of expansion, either actually or potentially.

This expansionism, briefly described here, contains several implications for the American understanding of life and death. Expansion is not regarded as a natural state of affairs, as the Romantics saw it. It is something that man causes to occur. It requires the full employment of man's resources. There is so much to learn and to experience in life and such potentiality for continued learning and enjoyment that the totality of man's energy is expended in the expanding sphere of life. The good life is the expanding life with its new experiences, new satisfactions, new mastery of erstwhile mysteries.

This is not to say that expansionism in itself is wrong. Progress is dependent upon sustained expansion. However, this point of view can become so dominant in its influence upon the value structure of a society that only that which involves tangible expansion is regarded as having worth. All else represents stagnation and loss. It might be presumed that death with its inevitable novelty would represent a challenging prospect for expansionism. Why should not man, who is geared to expanding existence, look to death as a new horizon? But at this very point the desirability of expansion halts because the necessary element of control is absent. The last frontier is reached and immediately loses its attraction. Consequently, it is necessary to separate the manageable areas for expansion from those which are beyond control. Expansionism thus demands that life and death be held apart.

Assumed Invulnerability

The expansionism of the frontier was fraught with risk. The possibility of confronting an insurmountable antagonist is always present. Such a crisis would be so disastrous, because expansion would halt and values would be lost, that man seeks to defend himself against it. One of his most formidable means of protection is an assumed invulnerability. This can take the form of a manifest destiny interpretation of history, a soldier's conviction that only a "bullet with my number on it" can do him harm, or an "it can't happen here" optimism.

Some of this assumed invulnerability is undoubtedly a part of human experience per se. Hocking reflects: "Man is the only animal that contemplates death, and also the only animal that shows any sign of doubt of its finality. This does not mean that he doubts it as a future fact. He accepts his own death, with that of others, as inevitable, plans for it, provides for the time when he shall be out of the picture. Yet, not less today than formerly, he confronts this fact with a certain incredulity regarding the scope of its destruction." [3] Man knows that he is only assuming invulnerability, that he is ultimately vulnerable, and yet to admit this fact totally is to be defenseless.

A similar theme is found in the writings of Freud when the personal and international tragedies produced by the First World War turned him to a consideration of man's view of death. Death occurs in war and peace, and man cannot escape from experiencing at some time or other grief for the dead. Such bereavement does cause man to consider his own mortality, even to imagine his own death. But, Freud points out, there is a certain protection because even when man imagines his own dying, he knows that he remains as the thinking subject. Man can think about his death but he cannot contemplate total annihilation. The fact that he can continue to remember the deceased causes him to conceive of a continuing existence beyond apparent death. These thoughts led Freud to conclude: "At bottom no one believes in his own death, or to put the same thing in another way, in the unconscious everyone of us is convinced of his own immortality." [4]

[3] William Ernest Hocking, *Thoughts on Death and Life* (New York: Harper & Brothers, 1937), p. 5.
[4] Sigmund Freud, "Thoughts for the Times on War and Death" (1915), *Collected Papers* (New York, Basic Books, 1959), IV, 305.

We recognize that this is much the same line of reasoning that led Borkenau to describe the assumption of immortality as a death-defying stand. Yet here we are speaking of assumed invulnerability as death-denying. Basically, the difference is this: one who accepts the Christian understanding of resurrection faces up to the fact of death. Resurrection is not assumed to come except through death. The assumed invulnerability of which we speak in examining contemporary life takes the pattern, not of defiance, but of denial. It has its structure of meaning so centered in life as it is now that it cannot even face up to the reality of death.

An excellent illustration of this is seen in the current refusal of millions of Americans to change their smoking habits in the light of modern medical research findings. In spite of seemingly incontrovertible evidence linking incidence of cancer with cigarette smoking, after a momentary dip cigarette sales have risen to higher levels. Why is it that countless individuals assume that they are invulnerable to cancer or death from cancer? It is not their belief in resurrection or immortality that causes them to defy death. It seems much more accurate to assert that they deny death and risk vastly increased chances for shortening life rather than curtail immediate satisfaction. Expressed in the vernacular, "living it up" is more important than living.

Life and death are separated by the assumption of invulnerability. Man's energy is devoted to living and to his unconscious, irrational denials of the possibility of his destruction by death.

Vitalism

Another feature of the American view of life is vitalism, the supreme valuation of vitality. Our public structure of values places a distinct premium on the life of a vigorous individual who is filled with boundless youthful energy. Although his work may be cerebral, he demonstrates his true vitality through sports and physical activity. The ideal person is regarded as aggressive, outgoing, gregarious, pouring vitality into social relationships. Productivity is one of the most important criteria for assessing worth. A successful man will be sufficiently vigorous to produce results in his work and in turn to provide a growing income for the support and advancement of his family. A successful woman will employ her energy in remunerative employment, in advancing and improving the status of her family, and in community activities.

Similarly our society devalues passivity and interprets inactivity as weakness. The man on the street commonly views as a "freeloader" the artist or the intellectual whose labors can scarcely be measured by the usual norms of productivity. The person whose full powers are limited by illness, handicap, or age is often an object of disdain, or at best pity, unless he can overcome his obstacles to demonstrate his capacity to produce. Lack of productive accomplishment is taken as a mark of inferiority or deficiency. Leisure, unless it is earned by producing, is frowned upon as indolence or waste.

The cornerstone of such a value system is vitality, liveliness. Life is interpreted largely in physical terms. Very often the picture is one-dimensional, giving attention only to surface vitality without probing the wealth of the deeper resources of character, reflection, and experience.

The vitalism that affects the American view of life and death is aptly illustrated by the way in which aging is regarded. The kind of vigor which is regarded as necessary for the good life is associated with the younger years of life. Thus there is a tendency to look down upon the aging process, because it involves the depletion of this essential resource. Unbelievably large amounts of energy, time, and money are devoted to efforts to keep young or to appear young. A veritable cult of exercisers has grown from the identification of health with youthful vigor. Advertising has produced millions of sales by suggesting that commodities are for those who would look, act, or "think" young. In spite of the fact that he is just as anomalous as an infantile adult, in our society the acceptable older person is the one who appears and acts young. The unacceptable are more and more segregated from the mainstream of economic and social life. Even in the home the basic social structure of the American family involves only two generations. There is no common pattern, either patriarchal or matriarchal, in which the third generation plays a significant role. Truly in this way of life the race belongs to the swift and the battle to the strong.

One of the reasons for the denial of the values which can be found in aging is that aging and death are related. Normally it is in the later years of life that the point occurs where life and death are juxtaposed. The close association of old age and death stirs the fear of aging, which is closely akin to the fear of dying. "Herman Feifel shows that a primary subconscious concern of the person over fifty, as revealed through projective testing, is preoccupation with his own death." [5] A number of other studies indicate that reflective concern about dying is related to the developmental age of the person. Because of the threatening nature of this process, many individuals deny it to consciousness. A part of their evasion is the struggle to maintain youthful vitality in spite of the inexorable advance of old age.

It is in what we have called vitalism that the effort to separate life from death reaches absolute proportions. Vitalism requires that life be narrowly or partially defined. It is seen only in terms of strength, growth, vigor. The negative aspect of life must be avoided at all cost. It must not be acknowledged that living and dying are always parallel courses, that we not only live but also die in the process of development.

[5] Margaretta Bowers, et al., Counseling the Dying (New York: Thomas Nelson and Sons, 1964), p. 2.

Vitality is frankly regarded as the *summum bonum*, the repository of all that has value. So commanding is this attractive valuation of living that no effort need be made to find any value in death nor to confront any present values with the positive reality of death. Public sentiment is much more favorably inclined toward heroic medical treatment for the hopelessly ill than toward euthanasia. Art forms dealing with death, such as Picasso's "Guernica," are often regarded as "way out" morbidity.

Materialism

Another aspect of the contemporary American view of life is the materialism that dominates our thinking. Here we are not speaking at all in a pejorative sense, implying greed or crassness. Rather we refer to materialism as a life view which establishes meaning only on the basis of material things, which regards reality as limited to material objects. For the materialist nothing more than the material is involved in life. The material context provides a substantial reality which is palpable and empirically verifiable.

In a somewhat more superficial sense materialism causes one to find his own personal meaning enhanced by the value of those material things which he can call his own. The status symbols of each generation fulfill this function as a sense of worth is found in possession. Reading the advertisements for automobiles readily reveals the potency of the appeal, not just to have a more adequate car, but to be a more important person.

Materialism is uncongenial to the thought of death for a variety of reasons. Death represents dissolution of the body, the material structure in which a man's life is lived. Thus it is conceived as the negation of reality. This negation is resisted by seeking to maintain some tangible part of the person,

31

some object through which the reality of the person who dies is preserved.

In similar fashion, death is apparently the termination of relationship to material things which have imputed value to the possessor. Death thus becomes the destroyer of value and must be denied. The old adage, "You can't take it with you," is devastating to one whose self has been affirmed only on the basis of ownership or control.

But, it might be argued, there are instances where the death of another actually increases one's possessions. Would this not neutralize the threat of death for the materialist because it would enhance his worth? Even under such circumstances death is regarded with tremendous ambivalence. Freud pointed out that a person may be very anxious about the death of another, particularly if he stands to gain by that death, because his anticipation of gain may be unconsciously construed as a wish for the death to take place. Assumptions of personal omnipotence remaining from infantile stages of development may create the impression that wishing the death in some way brought the death to pass. So powerful inhibitions are enforced against even thinking about the demise of one from whose death there would be profit. Again a pattern of evasion is called forth.

The single fixation of values upon the material elements of life, regardless of the form it may take, necessitates the separation of life from death because death represents dissolution and negation of the only basis of true worth.

Optimism

There is an inherent optimism present in the American view of life which also bears upon our considerations. Recognizing that we are speaking in broad, transpersonal terms, the prevailing tone of life has been one of prosperity and progress. The achievement of rapid growth, tremendous business, industrial and scientific development, abundant natural and human resources have created a sense of well-being. Under the influence of such a climate of success there develops a tendency to minimize anything negative. Prosperity becomes an anesthetic which dulls the senses to the sharp edges of tragedy and hardship. Belief in progress becomes an escape from the difficulties arising out of limitation and deficiency.

With the possible exception of several wars and some periods of economic depression, America has been spared major tragedy. It has never known the impact of wars that lasted for decades, it is unacquainted with plagues and famines that decimated the population. It has not endured lengthy occupations by hostile forces nor political bloodbaths. Its optimism has not been tempered by national tragedy.

This is not to say that individuals and minorities have not suffered tragedy. The point is that the American view of life leaves them ill prepared to deal with tragedy. There is no national paradigm of death and new life such as the experiences of postwar Germany or of the Jewish people. In a sense the American view of life is like that of the middle-class adolescent who is so filled with the exuberance of youth that thoughts of suffering and tragedy are remote from his mind. The American tradition is not really in a position to prepare an individual to cope with the negative dimensions of life as well as the positive. Consider, for example, the difficulty encountered even by liberal Caucasians in understanding the depth of the suffering of the Negro.

Life is commonly viewed superficially, with little regard for the richness and depth which might be apprehended if its tragic dimensions were also seen and understood. Under such circumstances death cannot be seen in meaningful relationship to life. It represents a potential foreign body in a way of life. It must be ignored as long as possible by restricting the vision to *la dolce vita*. So people avoid thinking of or talking about their own death. They try to divert the thoughts of those who

33

must themselves face the imminent possibility of dying. It is almost as if the prevailing optimism were regarded as so fragile that the acknowledgment of some discordant note would break the spell.

Time Sense

The American sense of time also has its effect upon the view of life and death. We know that the time sense of an individual shifts in various stages of the process of his development. The infant lives on the narrow edge of the present, seeking immediate satisfaction of his present needs. The child begins to relate past experience to the present in the process of learning. The adolescent rebels against the past and is sensitized to the future, although he is ambivalent toward both. His state of flux is so difficult that he alternately clasps the past and grasps the future. The mature adult is meaningfully oriented in all of the dimensions of time. The aged person has a nostalgic relationship to the past, is limited in exploiting the present, and has begun to be at peace with the future.

The time sense of the American culture seems to be akin to that of the late adolescent. American man acknowledges the past as important but is not much bound to it. He smiles indulgently at the anachronisms that he sees in the strong traditions of older cultures. It is the present that is regarded as the truly meaningful sphere of existence. He is both hopeful and anxious about the future, which he regards as meaningful largely as it flows into the present.

The immediate future can be dealt with because it is manageable. So in life one does think ahead to make such provision as he can for the future. He seeks education which prepares for gainful employment, he participates in retirement plans, and provides insurance protection. Thus he is not oblivious to the future and its needs. But once these are taken care of, the concern for the future is greatly diminished. Note the way in which all these plans for the future are related to the foreseeable present. They have to do only with the future flowing into the present. They do not really conceive of the future in an extended sense.

Death cannot be seriously regarded in such a view of the future, because death renders the future unmanageable. It negates time, not in the sense of making time stand still as is the aim of pleasure, but as the ending of time. Because time is regarded as having meaning only when it is related to the present; death, as the annihilation of time, must be separated from life.

Anxiety

Our era has been described by Auden as the age of anxiety, a phenomenon which must be related to our understanding of life and death. Many of the elements of the culture which have just been described have touched upon the production of anxiety. Death plays a part in this anxiety, whether it be the hovering crisis of potential thermonuclear destruction or the subconscious preoccupation of the middle-aged with his own demise.

The fear of death has always been a potent force in man. Archaeological evidence indicates that man, even in prehistoric times, was concerned with the problem. Efforts were made to resuscitate the dead, to simulate life, to prevent the movement of malevolent spirits. Fear of death took the form of fear of the dead. Soon the death of another became a reminder of man's own mortality. As Schopenhauer pointed out, with the emergence of man's reason came the shocking certainty that he himself would die.

Anxiety causes man to seek to defend himself. Usually this takes one of two possible courses: either one seeks to avoid the anxiety-producing threat or one seeks to gain control over that which threatens. Both of these defensive mechanisms can be seen in use against the threat of death in our culture.

The pattern of avoidance is quite obvious in the American understanding of death. Euphemisms such as "expired" or "passed away" are preferred to the frank recognition that a person has "died." Serious conversation about death is taboo. From the time of childhood individuals are insulated in every way possible from the face and reality of death. Complex disguises are arranged to convert mortuary customs into a grand deceit. Often efforts are made to eliminate completely any contact with the body of the deceased. As we have already pointed out, there is a consistent turning away from all signs and indications of the reality of death. Even the popular delight in humor that is attached to funerals, cemeteries, and undertakers can be understood as a way of spoofing the reality of death by making it ludicrous or trivial. If one can laugh at something, it hardly needs to be feared as tragic. In all of these ways the defense of avoidance is manifest.

Even more basic to those evasive patterns are the ways in which death is removed from consideration as a part of life. Men have found that it is painful to admit the reality that death is an inescapable human condition. They strive to circumvent this admission by depicting death as the result of accidental, rather than necessary, circumstances or as an intrusion into the natural order of life.

In a way accidental death is more easily tolerated than so-called natural death. Of course, the suddenness of accidental death is traumatic for the bereaved. But in terms of the way in which an individual's death reminds others of their own mortality, accidental death actually tends to soften the impact. The inference to be drawn from an accident is that it could have been avoided or prevented. The circumstances of any particular accident are not really too important here. The crucial matter is the implication that death is preventable. An accident need not be regarded as a necessary or inevitable part of human existence. Thus the ultimate significance of death for man is reduced. Seeing death as an accident also is an effort to deny for death a meaning. An accident is random, unplanned, purposeless. Since life is regarded as purposeful and death seen in this way is without meaning, there is ample justification for keeping death totally separate from life.

Much the same is true of a view of death which interprets it as an intrusion upon life. Death cannot be totally disregarded because it occurs with devastating regularity. But as an intrusion, it can be regarded as irrelevant to life. It is foreign and disconnected totally from living. Thus it is perfectly justifiable to concentrate all energy and thought upon life without giving death any attention. Life can be lived in detachment from the reality of death because they are not seen as having any common ground in existence.

The other major defense against anxiety-producing death is control. Instead of theological and philosophical interpretations, death is defined as a medical problem. It is the ultimate illness. It can be investigated scientifically and, in a sense, treated. Just as birth control is a medical reality, so too there is a growing implication that death control is possible. Major reductions in infant mortality, mass inoculations to immunize against dread diseases of the past, and dramatically increasing longevity are elements in the medical effort to control death. Serious reflection shows, however, that scientific medicine can delay death but cannot do away with it. The control of death is still very much limited.

But even limited medical control of death can be employed as a defense to avoid confrontation of death as reality. Awareness of limited control can fairly easily escalate to the stance which I described earlier as assumed invulnerability. The knowledge that modern man is developing the capacity to deal with death scientifically is sufficient to provide him with a defense against the fact that he cannot control it ultimately.

One might assume that, as has been true in other areas,

man's ability to change the course of nature would make him more and more open to an understanding of nature. With death this has not been the case. Rather than gaining confidence for the confrontation of death, man has used his capacity for limited control as another means for avoiding reality, for not seeing death as intimately related to life. The protection and prolongation of life has apparently served only to increase the need for defending oneself against consideration of dying.

Confronting Death in Our Time

Some few voices from a variety of quarters are raised against these defensive efforts to deny, avoid, or control death. They point to the necessity for confronting death, for seeing it in intimate relationship to life. They refuse to join in the grand deceit.

Some of these voices are found in the great literature and drama of our day. For example, Miller's *Death of a Salesman* protests illusion, delusion, and escapism in American life. The death of Willie Loman began long before the suicidal crash of his car. It was closely related to all of his living. Death was neither intrusion nor accident but came as an integral part of the tragic life of the Lomans.

The writings of Hemingway repeatedly bring life into face-to-face relationship with death. Death cannot be separated from life, because it is only in confronting death as reality that man really begins to live. The moment where life and death join is the real moment of truth. Every issue and meaning in life draws together at this single point. Evasion would be life's greatest loss.

Contrast these two examples of American authors who speak out for the honest encounter of death as a part of life with the shallow and sterile treatment given to death in the writings of Spillane or the movies of Hitchcock. In those portrayals one has the typical American view of death as intrusion. It has no logic, no meaning, no realness. The American mind can tolerate virtually unlimited quantities of violent death in chronicles of the Old West, private-eye cases, and personal tales of horror, so long as they are easily recognized as fictional and not truly related to life. In fact, it might be maintained that the reader of such superficial treatments of death obviates his deeper consideration of mortality by toying with death as unreality. The truly profound literature of our age will not permit this evasion.

Contemporary psychology has also spoken out against the pattern of avoidance. Taking their cue from Freud, who saw preparation for death as the best means for enduring life, Lindemann, Feifel, Bowers, Eissler, and others contribute a great deal to our understanding of the way in which the human psyche is able to deal best with death. They are unanimous in pointing to the psychological difficulties that ensue when man is not prepared to cope with loss and death.

If death is totally separated from life, there is little possibility that the meaning found in life can have any bearing on the meaning given to death. Growing interest in the potentiality of psychotherapy for the dying[6] is based on this possibility. The dying person is helped to confront the meaning of what is transpiring in his experience within the context of the meaning of his entire life. A new honesty and authenticity develops which does not avoid death but rather enables the person to die with the dignity of meaning.

Philosophy has always been concerned with death and dying. Existentialism, one of the leading philosophical thrusts of our era, demands that man confront both life and death, both being and nonbeing. Death is a part of being. As soon as one exists he is thrown into the possibility of nonbeing (i.e.,

[6] Margaretta Bowers, et al., Counseling the Dying; K. R. Eissler, The Psychiatrist and the Dying Patient (New York: International Universities Press, 1955).

dying). For Heidegger the acceptance of the inevitable possibility of one's own death is the impetus for truly authentic living. This process is called running ahead to one's own death in thought. Neither life nor death under such circumstances can be peripheral. Man is plunged to the core of his existence by the realization that he will die. Everything trivial and false drops away. However, this can never happen if true living is evaded by a false separation of life and death.

A slightly different tack is taken by another leading existentialist, Sartre. Because he regards both life and death as absurdities, he lacks Heidegger's certainty that in facing death one can find meaning for life. This could be, according to Sartre, only if man could choose the time of his dying. Death then does not show the real meaning of being but only reveals man's freedom. As man poises on the abyss of death he knows what freedom is. In this moment alone, in acknowledging the possibility of dying, does man rise above the absurdity. Sartre does bring life and death together. But note that he does so with the insistence that man needs to assert control over death in order to have the burden of existence lightened.

Contemporary philosophy no longer finds satisfactory the Platonic understanding that death is the great release from the prison of life into the world of pure spirit. Man's present understanding of existence regards both life and death, being and nonbeing, with horror and despair. It is difficult to find meaning in either one. Thus little reason exists for keeping life and death separate.

A somewhat more positive appeal for the confrontation of death as reality comes from the Christian religion. A great deal of American thinking has been founded upon a heritage of Western Christian thought. This is true of the traditional American understanding of death. This view has seen both life and death as taking place within the context of God's purposeful action. Just as God is regarded as the creator of life, so too he draws life to its close. Although it should not be conceived in simple cause and effect terms, this process has been regarded as distinctly personal, a part of man's relationship to God. By some, life was understood as a probationary or preparatory period which was concluded by death. Death was purposeful because it became a prelude to a new life. According to the Christian understanding, death and resurrection must be considered together because the possibility of the latter changes entirely the context for understanding the former.

It is the Christian position that life, death, and life after death must be hopefully grounded in God's action. All three elements of existence are related to God's will and God's power. Christianity has rejected with consistency an understanding of man's immortality as confidence in an indomitable part of his nature and has preferred to think of life after death as resurrection, new life bestowed by God's mercy.

This basic Christian structure has often been reinterpreted or contorted in American thought. Totally secular hopes and aspirations have been infused into the hope for life after death, anticipating freedom from slavery, poverty, care, anonymity. Crude, unwarranted materializations have been concocted. While one might regret these excessive interpretations, they do not really alter the basic fact that acceptance of life after death enables one to confront death.

Earlier I spoke of Borkenau's delineation of death-accepting and death-defying attitudes. The Christian understanding of resurrection can be regarded as death-defying. Perhaps the comparison of the deaths of Socrates and of Jesus made by Cullmann[7] will point to the relevance of Borkenau's distinction for the Christian view. Socrates and Jesus confronted death in widely different ways. According to Plato's description, Socrates sat calmly with his friends speaking of immortality. He accepted death as a means for the release of his soul from

[7] Oscar Cullmann, *Immortality of the Soul or Resurrection of the Dead?* (London: Epworth Press, 1958), pp. 23 f.

its earthly prison. He regarded survival as inherent in his nature; therefore, he could accept death as a friend. Jesus, on the other hand, died in anguish. Death was a frightful horror —no friend, but the last enemy. In death he felt utterly forsaken by God. Yet Christians believe that he overcame death. A vital part of this conviction is that he overcame death *by dying*. This was not a victory of not dying, wholly or in part. The acceptance of death here is in defiance rather than in acquiescence.

This has become the basis for Christian insistence that death must be faced rather than being detached from life and avoided. It must, however, be admitted that this insistence has been less heeded by American thought than the much more easily accepted assumptions of an automatic survival of man's spirit.

There have been more profound challenges than this to the Christian view. The Freudian understanding of assumptions of immortality as man's necessary defense against the horror of dying has been a basis for calling the Christian understanding into question. The only possible rejoinder seems to be that the Freudian position is no more amenable to objective validation than is the Christian conviction.

The challenges of the secular scientific viewpoint which understands life and death only in empirical terms challenges the Christian understanding of the nature of life and death. Mortality is regarded as a fact which has no metaphysical significance. Human death, except for the emotional consequences for those related to the deceased, is practically no different than the death of any other living thing. Fulton again speaks to this situation.

Our present position, designated by Borkenau as the modern post-Christian attitude, with its disintegration of belief in immortality, is seen as standing on the threshold of a nihilistic philosophy of despair and denial. Modern secularism seems bent upon a historical course that has as its outcome the denial of the relevance, possibly the existence, of self to the end that death itself, finally, is defeated.[8]

The way in which this challenge abets the death-denying approach so characteristic of our culture is obvious.

The Christian faith has not been oblivious to the terror of death nor has it minimized the struggle involved in dying. It has consistently urged that death be regarded openly and realistically. No effort has been made to define death as something that is unnatural and detached from life's natural processes. Life and death must be seen together in the light of the Christian faith in the resurrection. The Christian church, on the basis of its own faith, adds its voice to the call that the understanding of life and death be joined and that evasion, avoidance, and futile efforts to control death be abandoned in favor of authentic confrontation.

In this chapter I have sought to indicate that the American attitude toward death is often naïve and superficial. It reflects a shallowness which is to be found also in the American view of life. Failing to find any deep meaning of life beyond sensate values, the modern American has shielded himself from discovery of any profound understanding of death. He has obviated such discovery by totally divorcing life from death, focusing his total energy and resources on living. The question then arises: What is the relationship between this popular understanding of life and death and our funeral customs and practices?

[8] Robert L. Fulton, "Death and the Self," *Journal of Religion and Health,* July, 1964, p. 361.

3

Modern Man and
the Funeral

The transition from the unified understanding of life and death to a dissociated, separated understanding and the investment of all meaning in life have exerted a number of influences on the contemporary funeral. The development of a view of life such as that described in chapter 2 has tended to skew the funeral from a number of its original purposes and has brought a new set of values into the funeral.

The funeral, once seen as a ritual which conveyed the meanings that surround the juncture of life and death, often has come to reflect the patterns of avoidance and control, the two devices modern men employ to keep life and death apart. The funeral reflects the values cherished by the culture, but we must not forget that the funeral also can exert an influence upon cultural values. Although we shall give our attention here to ways in which the funeral has accommodated itself to the culture, it is our ultimate purpose to suggest ways in which the funeral can be a means for changing the pattern of modern man's thoughts on life and death.

Patterns of Avoidance

There are numerous funeral practices in our time which constitute efforts to avoid the reality of death and the painfulness of the experience of mourning. Very few of these avoidance mechanisms belong to the basic and traditional structure of the funeral itself. Most of them are seen in customs and practices which have accrued in recent decades on the periphery of the funeral. They have, however, tended to move from the periphery into the essential fabric of the funeral itself.

EMOTIONAL SUPERFICIALITY

The funeral has never been an occasion that was divorced from the emotions of the participants. The poignancy of separation from a loved one by death normally is too dramatic to be ignored completely.

There have been periods in our history when the view of the relationship of life and death was such that death could be openly and honestly faced. Sorrow was not minimized, nor was shallow comfort given. The individual was deeply saddened by the death of a relative or friend, but he bore this grief in open acknowledgment of the presence of death in the midst of life.

However, it must also be admitted that there was a time when funerals played harshly upon the emotions, crudely stimulating and manipulating sorrow, guilt, fear. These practices are now generally rejected both for their needless morbidity and for the way in which they deprived the individual mourner of his freedom by evoking a response of synthetic rather than authentic feeling.

In reaction to the stimulation of raw feelings and reflecting the need for accommodating the increasing desire for avoidance, the funeral assumed a new emotional tone. Since it would be impossible to deny emotional expression altogether, the course of superficiality has become a suitable means for avoiding the profound emotions involved in bereavement. The response can be made to sentimental words, soft lights, and tremulous music rather than to the reality of death drawn near. Some emotional outlet is provided, but it is carefully regulated by its synthetic stimuli.

The average American appears to be quite fearful of plumbing the emotional depths of his living. The expression of authentic deep feeling is uncommon. Perhaps it is due to fear of the uncontrollable potency of deep emotion that contemporary Americans discipline their responses so severely. Emotions can be expressed acceptably only by indirection. Hostility cannot be openly expressed, but it is indirectly discharged through vicarious experience of acts of violence in TV westerns, mystery novels, and boxing matches. Love often cannot be expressed or experienced directly, so it is superficially and vicariously sought in the romantic entanglements of stage and screen and the revelations of the private passions of public figures which cover the newsstands. Avoiding depth in life is the natural companion of avoidance of the deeper meanings of death. The profound experiences of separation by death and the confrontation of the reality of death itself are too much for a people unschooled in the direct experiencing of authentic feelings. So death is shrouded in an air of unreality, dividing it from the reality of life with an insulating barrier of illusion. Separation from the deceased is supposedly rendered less painful by covering it with an aura of sentiment.

What, then, are some of the things one finds in contemporary funerals that betray the avoidance of profound apprehension of reality and the substitution of superficiality? The affirmations of the reality of death found in traditional orders for the burial of the dead are often replaced or smothered by poetic suggestions that death is unreal, that it only seems to have taken place, that it is a somewhat inconsequential automatic transition from one stage of existence to another. At times this represents a sincere, although misguided, effort to convey the Christian meaning of death. Unfortunately, all too often it mistakes the death-defying qualities of the Christian faith for death denial. Or to illustrate further, the musical accompaniment of the funeral service often employs techniques which convey further unreality. The tremulant chords of an electronic organ or wavering notes of recorded chimes provide the mood music of illusion, supporting the theme of musical compositions which describe with appropriate vagueness beautiful isles of somewhere and ivory palaces. Compare these with the strong affirmations of Bach's "Come, Sweet Death" or the hymn "For All the Saints Who from Their Labors Rest."

Because the arousing of superficial emotional reactions is brought about by techniques closely related to the development of conditioned reflexes, the implication would be that once the stimuli are no longer present, the response is no longer evoked. Take away the shallow sentiment, the artificial solemnity, the ethereal music, and the emotional expressions vanish with them. The presence of some superficial feelings, successfully limited to a brief period and a specific place, has satisfied the expectation that something should be felt and expressed at such a time. But a truly profound encounter with the meaning of death for life is obviated. The funeral thus may not be permitted to carry out one of its very important functions of enabling the individual honestly to confront his loss as reality while supported by the concern of a community which in part shares his loss. The finding of meaning in life by facing the meaning of death is made extremely difficult.

ILLUSIONS OF LIFE

Somewhat more obvious components of patterns of avoidance which have arisen in funeral practices are the efforts to create the illusion of life. The unspoken assumption seems to be that the reality of death is disguised if the illusion of life can be sustained.

Experience indicates again and again that it is possible to do the right thing for the wrong reason. The preparation of the body of the deceased for viewing is illustrative of this point. The embalming, dressing, and application of cosmetics which are a part of this preparation can have two functions. These things can be a part of the normal process of "improving on nature" to which we are all willing daily accomplices. Combing hair, shaving, permanent waves, lipstick, girdles, shoulder padding, and dentures constitute everyday efforts to improve the natural state of affairs and to ready oneself for public appearance. Since viewing the body of the deceased is one of the ways in which the reality of the situation can be reinforced, it seems quite acceptable that the person should be made to appear somewhat as he did in life. On this basis there would seem to be no more objection to the application of cosmetics to the dead body, for example, than there is to the improvement of appearance in life.

However, we must recognize that there is a difference between preparation of the body to improve appearance and preparation designed to create the illusion of life. The intention should be to make the dead body presentable, not to cover up death.

This is carried to further lengths by the custom in some funeral establishments of having the body first viewed by the family as if the deceased were merely asleep. The body is attired in pajamas or negligee and placed in a tastefully furnished bedroom setting. So completely is the illusion maintained that one pastor reported that when he called at a mortuary he was told, "Mrs. X will see you now," as if the corpse were receiving guests.

Sometime the accouterments of burial are so described as to convey the illusion of continuing life. The comfort of the deceased or his well-being becomes a concern in the presentation of caskets with innerspring mattresses or burial vaults which endlessly defy the ravages of the elements.

REMOVAL FROM ORDINARY LIFE

Still another avoidance pattern involves the separation of the funeral from the everyday experience of life. Rather than seeking to relate the important events which surround the death of a loved one to the broad range of experience that constitutes life, a pattern of isolation into the realm of the extraordinary has evolved.

The place where the funeral is conducted provides an illustration of this fact. There are certainly some valid reasons in given instances for having the funeral in a funeral home rather than in the home of the deceased or the church to which he belonged. Considerations of convenience, accessibility, and appropriateness are legitimate bases for some individuals to prefer holding the funeral in a funeral home. On the other hand, it is also possible that this is a device for avoiding confrontation of the reality of the situation.

Selection of a place which is reserved exclusively for funerals may well be a way of trying to isolate this experience from the rest of living. Pastors sometimes encounter families who indicate that they do not wish to have the funeral in the church because they fear that they will always associate unhappy memories with the church building. On much the same basis as the observation of a taboo, the localization of the funeral away from the familiar sites of living helps to strengthen the efforts at avoidance by keeping the everyday areas of life untouched by the reality of death.

MINIMIZED PERSONAL INVOLVEMENT

Quite related to the avoidance mechanism just described is the minimizing of personal involvement which characterizes much of today's funeral practice. Confrontation of the reality of death can be escaped by remaining as detached as possible from participation in the activities required by death and the funeral.

Within the last several generations the preparation of the dead and the arrangement of the funeral has become almost exclusively the responsibility of the funeral director. One of the inevitable results of specialization is that people become less and less involved in the services that are performed for

49

them. In many situations no dramatic problems are posed by this remoteness. However, if delegation of responsibility to specialists becomes a means for evading reality, serious consequences may result. So, if giving over to the funeral director all necessary action called for when death occurs enables a detachment of the mourner from the reality of the crisis of death, a disservice may be performed. It is highly unlikely that we shall ever revert to the pattern of earlier days and take back from the specialist the functions of preparing the dead and arranging the funeral. But if such delegation of responsibility becomes a means of getting death out of sight or of remaining as detached as possible from the whole process, no good purpose is served.

Another variation of this same minimization of involvement is often seen in a different aspect of the funeral. Many pastors make a studied effort to impersonalize the funeral under the mistaken notion that pain is lessened for the mourners by approaching the funeral with total objectivity. Ministers will describe their efforts to reduce personal references to the deceased, to minimize any mention of association with the deceased, in order to avoid emotion in the mourner. In the survey described earlier only 39 percent of the ministers indicated that they normally made personal references to the deceased in their funeral sermons, and only 27 percent stated that they used a purely factual obituary in the service. In other words, it is quite possible that many funeral services literally make no mention of the person who has died nor of the relationships that have been sustained with the deceased. Some of this objectivity is due to a perfectly legitimate desire to avoid the pitfalls of lavish eulogies, but all too often it represents an effort to minimize the painful personal involvement of the mourner in recalling his past experience with the deceased, thus circumventing his encounter with the reality of death.

Time also plays a part in seeking to reduce personal involvement. Various societies have established periods ranging from a few days to a year or more during which mourners follow certain prescribed patterns of behavior designed to enable their readjustment to life. In America the period of structured mourning has steadily been shortened. In contrast to the year of formal mourning of several generations ago, at the present time the recognized mourning period is informal and brief. Quite often it is limited to very little more than the time between the occurrence of death and the funeral. There is at present even some pressure to shorten the period between death and the funeral, which in many sections of the country is normally three days.

There is nothing sacrosanct about three days or seven days or thirty days. It does need to be said, however, that a structured period of mourning is intended to give the person time for confronting the reality of the situation in which he finds himself. The shorter the time allowed for this encounter with reality, the greater the likelihood that the individual will be minimally involved. The tendency to want to get the funeral over with and to return to life as usual as quickly as possible can readily become a part of the mechanism of avoidance.

Patterns of Control

Other funeral practices of our time can be seen as efforts to cope with death by controlling it. Already we have commented upon the creation of the illusion of life as a means for avoiding the reality of death. This illusion is also designed to imply a measure of control over death. If the person can be made to appear to be asleep, hopefully the painful reality of death is blunted. By making the results of this phenomenon appear to be temporary, death seems to be made more amenable to man's control. Thus by regulating appearances an effort is made to restrain the power of death. So long as the appearance of life can be maintained, death is held off.

PRESERVATION AS CONTROL

Possibly even more dramatic in our time is the effort to control death by seeking long-term preservation of the body of the deceased. The total annihilation which death presents is most tangibly conveyed in the dissolution of the body. Prevention of that dissolution can imply that the devastating power of death is at least partially held in check.

There is good evidence to support the value of the bodily presence of the deceased up to a point. Seeing the body in repose is one of the helpful ways in which the reality of the situation can be reinforced for the mourners. The presence of the corpse at the viewing and the funeral provides a tangible focus for the expression of the feelings of the mourners and the supportive community. But there should be no question that they see the body of one who has died. No effort need be made to imply that dissolution of the body will be postponed beyond the time of the funeral.

The value of the presence of the body of the deceased reaches the point of diminishing returns in a relatively short time. The reinforcement of reality that takes place in viewing the body can become, by extending the time of maintaining this bodily presence, a means for reinforcing unreality. The long-term preservation of the body becomes an effort to control death by preventing the body's dissolution. The funeral can provide a terminus for the viewing of the body of the deceased and can bring a sense of finality into focus. But efforts to preserve the body indefinitely beyond the time of the funeral can easily undo this sense of finality and imply a continuing body presence which actually deters the mourning process.

Embalming and the preparation of the body can be justified as a part of the process which enables the accomplishment of the useful purposes resulting from viewing the deceased. But to seek to justify the process as a means to long-term prevention of the dissolution of the body actually becomes a subtle effort to control death by preventing destruction of the body.

The extensive use of burial vaults may have some value in terms of cemetery maintenance by preventing the collapse of the grave some years following burial, but again there is no value in the assumption that encasing the body in a hermetically sealed container enables lasting preservation of the corpse. If there is the assumption that the body of the deceased maintains its presence in the grave, there is the possibility that the mourners will remain bound in a frustrating and morbid relationship to that assumed presence and will be deterred in the successful completion of their grief work.

In a sense these efforts to preserve the body indefinitely reflect something of the materialism of our day. Ultimate value is attached to that which has tangible reality, and the body is seen as the concrete reality of the person. These materialistic presuppositions would indicate that one can preserve the value of the person only by preventing the dissolution of the tangible body. This means of seeking to control the destruction that death brings becomes a matter of crucial concern.

CONTROLLING DISSOLUTION

From what has been said above it might be assumed that the logical way to avoid this neurotic effort to control death by long-term preservation of the body would be through the process of cremation. Here the dissolution of the dead body is accomplished in a short time rather than the extended time of natural dissolution. There is much to be said in support of this assumption. Cremation and suitable disposition of the ashes does convey the end of bodily presence and continued interpersonal relationship as they have been known.

However, we need to be reminded that cremation can also be motivated by a desire to control death. We recall that Sartre argued against Heidegger's theme that by running forward toward one's death in thought, one could find authentic meaning for life. Sartre insisted that this would be valid only if man had control over the time of his death. Meaning is found not in the possibility of death but in the freedom to control whether one lives or dies. This suggests that it would be possible to understand cremation as desirable not just as a means for facing the reality of death by enabling the rapid dissolution of the body. Cremation could also be construed as a means for controlling death by controlling the processes of dissolution rather than leaving these to nature.

My purpose is not to argue for or against cremation but to point out that it is subject to a variety of subtle understandings and motivations which need to be examined carefully.

CONTROLLING RITUAL

It must also be recognized that ritual in itself is a form of controlling death. Archaeological research and comparative studies of religions indicate that sacrifice was often considered an essential part of burial rituals. Animal bones commonly found in the grave sites of prehistoric men point to a feast which was part of the burial rites. The assumption is that sacrifice was a part of this ritual in an effort to appease or control the awesome forces which brought death. Such extremes as human sacrifice of slaves of a dead nobleman or members of the deceased's family, as in the Hindu practice of suttee, were parts of the ritual designed to control death and evil spirits.

In the Christian tradition this element of control is not totally lacking. The Christian faith affirms that death can be defied because its ultimate power has been brought under control by the power of God. According to the Protestant Christian understanding the conduct of the funeral itself has no salutary effect upon the deceased, nor does it minimize in any sense the consequences of his death. So the Christian funeral is not in itself properly viewed as a controlling ritual. Rather, it is the ritual affirmation of the control of death enabled through the hope of the resurrection.

However, for a sizable proportion of the American people who are not personally committed to the Christian faith, there is still a desire for a ritual accompaniment for the occurrence of death. In many such instances a funeral is planned, a minister is secured, even though there is no viable connection with any community of faith. Thus the outward form of a religious service is maintained without any particularly meaningful response to its content. Such a funeral may well be an endeavor to retain a measure of ritual control over death. Yet, because of the lack of Christian presuppositions, the ritual does not accomplish the desired purpose and thus lacks meaning. It may be that this understandable failure is the source of some of the contemporary complaints that the funeral is lacking in value.

Patterns of Extravagance

There are still other ways in which the contemporary American funeral reflects the modern understanding of life and death. It has been pointed out by both supporters and critics of the value of the funeral that it has often become an occasion for excessive expenditure. Some commentators have claimed that this extravagance is produced by funeral interests intent upon enlarging their own profit. Others see ostentation and extravagance in the funeral as one of the many indications of the status seeking that has become the American antidote for feeling less than a real person.

There are numerous reasons for the willingness of many families to pay for funerals that may be costlier than necessary. For some it is an extension of their high standard of living. They have sufficient means to pay for luxuries in all areas of life including the funeral. Others may be seeking to preserve or gain social status by conspicuous consumption. Still others may be seeking to communicate their love and respect for the deceased by providing a funeral that is obviously costlier than it needs to be. There are some who may seek to assuage their guilty feelings about the poor quality of their relationship to the deceased in life by making possible a costly funeral. The social unacceptability of expressing grief publicly may encourage expression of such feeling indirectly via expenditure, lavish display, and status seeking.

This variety of possible motivations for high expenditures for the funeral rests upon several features of the American view of life which I have discussed earlier. Obviously, there is a connection with the materialism of our time. The assumption is that the more a thing costs, the more it is worth, and the more a person is able to spend, the more worthwhile he is. This sounds ridiculously simple, and yet vast segments of our economy owe their very existence to such logic.

In a sense the separation of death from life which has come to characterize the American view is also a contributor to the high costs of funeral practices. This divorce of life and death requires that the reality of death be concealed or disguised. The subterfuges that are needed to sustain the illusion demand services which might otherwise be nonessential. All of the accouterments employed to make death seem unreal, all of the means by which long-term preservation of the corpse is sought, all of the superficial comforts of aestheticism cause an elaboration of the funeral and an increase in its costliness. Just as the extensive defenses of the psychotic individual cause him to expend tremendous amounts of psychic energy in shaping reality into a form he can handle, so the limited and unrealistic understanding of death in our time carries its own costliness.

Patterns of Reaction

As a result of the many currents of thought and feeling I have been describing, the funeral has lost some of its helpful purpose and intention. Instead of being a ritualized pattern for

56

coping with the reality of death and its implications for living, the funeral has in many ways been reshaped to perform quite different functions. Rather than providing an occasion for the recognition of loss and the effect of sundered relationships on the living, the funeral too often has blended into the patterns of denial of the reality of the situation. Rather than bringing to bear the full resources of a supporting community for the bereaved, the funeral has often tended to be increasingly privatized and insulated from group participation. Rather than providing a structure which sanctions and enables the work of mourning, the funeral has repeatedly become one of the many forces working for the repression of the authentic feelings of the bereaved.

The value of the funeral has been reduced as these helpful purposes have been neglected. It appears that the contemporary funeral often seeks to convey values which are so remote from its original intention that it has in many ways become something of an anomaly.

It is quite understandable then that in some quarters there has been a growing disillusionment regarding the funeral. Forms which were once meaningful and helpful seem no longer so because new motives have taken them over. This disillusionment is fairly widespread among clergymen and people of the church who sense that there is something wrong with the modern funeral but who may not always have sought to work out a detailed diagnosis of the problem.

A much more acute form of this reaction regards the funeral with cynicism. In our sophisticated age there is a general tendency toward deritualization. Being convinced of the meaninglessness of many modern rituals and being unaware of their former purposes and functions, some people find it easy to cast them aside. Without some basic grasp of the actual foundations of the funeral afforded in the understanding of death and mourning provided by psychology, sociology, cultural anthropology, and theology it is not difficult to discard the funeral as an outmoded form, a vestige.

There is also evidence in our time of a reaction to the funeral that might best be described as hostility. Man's anxieties about death and dying and the pain of mourning are so intense that there is a rejection of the funeral as a symbol of the reality of this suffering. Even the often diluted or contorted funeral of the present time has too much association with death to be acceptable. This threat is met with open opposition which sometimes takes the form of iconoclastic resistance to the funeral.

Far less dramatic than these is the bland acceptance of the status quo which characterizes another common reaction to the funeral. One goes through the motions of the funeral because it is the thing to do, but no particular value is derived other than the support which comes through conformity. Here again there is little appreciation of the original functions of the funeral or the purposes toward which it is presently directed. For the conformist the purpose of the funeral is irrelevant. This disregard for the function of the funeral is a strong contributor to many of the resistive reactions that have been described above.

There is also a reaction to the funeral which grows out of a desire to reform the funeral. This reaction takes various forms and directions depending on the criteria which are applied to the funeral. Some wish to reform the economic aspects of funeral practice. Some want to develop a sounder sociological or psychological basis for the funeral. Still others want to deepen the theological foundations for the funeral. Very few efforts at reform have cut across all of these approaches. Operating separately they run the extreme risk of canceling out one another's gains.

The most adequate reform of the funeral will grow out of the criteria applied by all these disciplines. Unless such an interdisciplinary approach is used, efforts to reform the funeral, to conserve its original functions, to extend new and meaning-ful functions, cannot succeed.

We have pointed out that the contemporary funeral has in many ways yielded to cultural pressures. It thoroughly reflects the dominant values of the culture.

The funeral can, however, be a means by which the attitudes of the culture toward death and mourning are reshaped. Ritual is not merely a passive reflector of cultural values; it also can participate in the structuring of these values. It is not impossible for the funeral to be restored to its basic purposes and functions and to exert a potent influence upon American thought and behavior. It can be a force in stemming the neurotic flight from reality of our time by affording the support that is necessary for the individual to confront death and loss realistically. It can undergird acceptance and defiance of death rather than the denying of death. It can resist the radical separation of death from life and deepen life's meaning by acknowledging the dramatic encounter with the reality of death.

This constructive and restorative treatment of the funeral is not a simple task. In order to indicate full appreciation of the difficulty of this project we must first examine the major critiques of the funeral in recent decades.

4

Analysis of Contemporary
Critiques of the Funeral

Like any socioreligious institution the funeral
has been subject to continual critical evaluation for many
centuries. The early Christian church continued many of the
practices of its day, while at the same time offering critical
interpretation of the pagan meanings of these customs. The
sketchy histories of funeral customs indicate in virtually every
era the maintenance of a tension between the church and
cultural practices surrounding death.

At times this tension was manifested through the stringent
application of a theological concept, such as a literal interpretation of the resurrection of the body which would make cremation undesirable or would urge burial of a Christian in conse-
crated ground. At other times the tension took the form of
criticism of status inequities, pride, ostentation, and inappropriate conduct at wakes and funerals.

Occasionally one finds legislation which was designed to
enforce a particular pattern of funeral observances. In 1681 the
Scottish Parliament, reflecting the austerity of the Scottish
Presbyterianism of that day, sought to limit the number of
persons who might attend the funeral of a person of rank to
one hundred and to forbid the carrying of branches, banners,
and other honors at church.[1] Other even more far-reaching

[1] Bertram S. Puckle, *Funeral Customs* (New York: Frederick A. Stokes
Company, 1926), p. 201.

measures are found in the 1645 "Directory for the Public Worship of God," where there is prohibition of kneeling or praying by or toward the dead corpse, reading or singing going to or at the grave. The position is stated in its most austere terms. "When any person departs this life, let the body be decently attended to from the house to the place for public burial and there immediately interred without any ceremony." [2]

Statements such as these represent the efforts of the church or the state to express critical evaluation of funeral practices. In our own time critiques of the funeral have more commonly taken the form of the report of the experience, investigation, and reflection of an individual.

The past decade has brought forth several strong critiques of the funeral. Whether one agrees wholly, partially, or not at all with these, serious analysis must be made. Such study will show how the critiques have pointed to profound problems connected with the funeral. Even more important for our purposes the critiques point up some of the serious difficulties encountered in attempting to evaluate the funeral. Since it is virtually a unanimous opinion of the critics that the funeral is a vestige, our effort to demonstrate value in the funeral, properly understood and conducted, must examine their stance rigorously and objectively.

The Forerunner

The basic pattern of modern critiques of the funeral was set in a volume which was widely read earlier in the twentieth century, Bertram Puckle's *Funeral Customs*. His deft satire is a precursor of some of the writings of more recent times.

Puckle offers an extremely interesting description of the development of many funeral customs. He does not document

[2] *Ibid.*, p. 244.

his study in such a way that the sources of his data in the writings of historians and anthropologists are easily traceable; still, there is a wealth of information (hopefully verifiable) to be found in his work.

In addition to description of the origin of funeral practices there is strong negative criticism. He sees funeral customs almost entirely as vestiges of superstitious fears and pagan practices, motivated largely by status desires, dread of the dead, and thoughtless repetition.

It cannot too strongly be insisted upon when we compare the practices of the past with the present, that the very customs to which we cling so unreasonably, are for the most part unworthy remnants of superstitious rites, and not anything dictated by any form of the Christian religion to which we may subscribe. This is important, because we can readily trace the continuity of such usages in the absence of any sort of authority for what we do—to the accepted and erroneous belief that they are associated in some way with the articles of faith, that it would be impious to roughhandle, thus they have been handed down from generation to generation, impervious even to ridicule and carefully fostered by The Dismal Trader.[3]

Puckle, writing in England, appears to have two major objectives. First of all, he seeks to demonstrate that the funeral is a totally outmoded social and religious phenomenon. He likens the funeral procession to a traveling circus. He sees vulgar minds finding occasions for transmuting nonentities into centers of attraction in the funeral ceremony. He lists fear of the dead as the origin for virtually every funeral custom, a fear that is the mark of a primitive and superstitious mind.

Presupposing that the funeral of his day is primarily a product of the commercial interests of the morticians, whom Puckle consistently dubs The Dismal Traders, he pours ridicule

[3] *Ibid.*, p. 32.

on them, their rusty black-coated minions and their round-rumped excuses for superior horseflesh. These become concrete targets for his objections to the funeral in general.

Puckle's investigation bears witness to the proliferation of features of the funeral ceremonies. It is quite possible that his claims of extravagance, ostentation, and superstition have substance. However, he states his thesis with great vigor: "When we have stripped any one of our funeral observances of its crapes and tinsel—those grave clothes of convention in which they have been preserved and embalmed—we shall find very little that is worthy of continuance." [4] He sees no positive value in funeral practices as he knows them. He bases this evaluation on his belief that primitive roots of some practices make the practices themselves necessarily pagan, that commercialization necessarily destroys value in a cultural phenomenon, that a desire to have needs met through receiving the attention of others is necessarily vulgar. Perhaps the findings of cultural anthropology, psychology, and pastoral theology in our day would tend to make his beliefs more sophisticated and his position less rigid.

A Sociological Critique

It was more than three decades before another major negative critique of the funeral was published: *The American Funeral*, by LeRoy Bowman.[5] Even though Bowman does not indicate particular awareness of the work which had been done by Lindemann, Rogers, Irion, and Jackson in the fields of psychiatry and pastoral theology,[6] he does seek to deal with the

---

[4] *Ibid.*, p. 253.

[5] *The American Funeral: A Study in Guilt, Extravagance and Sublimity* (Washington, D.C.: Public Affairs Press, 1959).

[6] Erich Lindemann, "Symptomatology and Management of Acute Grief," *The American Journal of Psychiatry*, CI (1944), 141-49; William F. Rogers, *Ye Shall be Comforted* (Philadelphia: Westminster Press, 1950); Paul E. Irion, *The Funeral and the Mourners* (Nashville: Abingdon Press, 1954); Edgar N. Jackson, *Understanding Grief* (Nashville: Abingdon Press, 1957).

funeral in the light of its psychological and theological dimensions as well as its sociological aspects. This marks a major forward step for negative critics of the funeral.

As a sociologist Bowman applied the methodology of his science to the study. He gained data through questionnaires and interviews with participants in funerals from many social and economic groups. Unlike virtually every other negative critic, Bowman discounts the satirical and humorous popularizing of the issues and individuals involved in the funeral. He correctly recognizes the very real possibility that such satire is often a way of hiding from one's own anxieties regarding death by seeking to reduce it to absurdity.

Bowman states the problem as he sees it in this way:

The American funeral appears to be an anachronism, an elaboration of early customs rather than the adaptation to modern needs that it should be.... Although anthropologists assign a positive function to the rite in primitive societies, no serious scientific effort has been made to ascertain whether a like function is served by the funeral in modern industrialized society.[7]

Although the funeral may have fulfilled a helpful function in a town and country society, a study of the funeral in the light of contemporary social change in family and community structure raises questions about its effectiveness and validity. The isolation of the individual in impersonal urban culture makes a communal expression of sorrow and support either unlikely or superficial. A bereaved family then, according to Bowman, is subject to several pressures. The depersonalization of the individual in mass culture causes mourners to try to use the funeral as a means for gaining esteem, status, group support. Yet, at the same time the funeral can no longer really supply these needs because of the busyness, the lack of relatedness of individuals. On this basis Bowman concludes that the Amer-

[7] Bowman, *The American Funeral*, p. vii.

ican funeral has become costly, ostentatious, and largely irrelevant to the needs of the bereaved.

There is also recognition of the way in which American culture has sought to avoid the harsh realities of life and death, the difficulty in facing death. Rather than assisting man to a deeper apprehension of the reality of death, the funeral, according to Bowman, has more and more participated in the conspiracy of evasion. Again this is interpreted as a sign of having outlived its usefulness.

The purpose of Bowman's critique appears to be twofold. First of all, he attacks the negative aspects of funeral practices, particularly commercialization, conspicuous display, and outmoded custom. The second emphasis is a positive attempt to suggest some new meanings for the funeral in the light of possible social and psychological values which might be found in it.

Bowman follows three major courses in his line of argument. He provides a detailed description and analysis of modern funeral practices. The funeral ritual is regarded as being traditionally in the province of the church. The growing secularism of our age makes this religious participation in the funeral a part of the anachronism which Bowman asserts. Although the funeral is regarded by the church as a part of its ministry, this service is received by many persons only as a custom observed because it is the "proper" thing to do. Bowman is not unsympathetic to the religious aspects of the funeral, but he does not see them as potent forces in the restoration or preservation of values in the funeral.

Something of the same pattern is described in terms of the social conditions which affect funeral practices. The homogeneity and solidarity of town and country America a generation ago afforded a structure in which the individual could find the support of a community that shared his experience. But recent decades have wrought considerable changes. The rapid mobility of our population, the gathering into massive urban societies, the patternless amalgamation of customs and traditions brought about an obliteration of meaningful forms for meeting the crises of death and bereavement. Bowman contends that a vacuum was thus created which has been filled by new customs that were designed and promulgated by commercial funeral interests. A rootless society has made possible rootless funeral practices, creating patterns of behavior that have more value to expansion of the funeral industry than in meeting needs of the mourners.

Bowman asserts that urbanization has reduced the possibility of real community to such an extent that the funeral no longer fulfills a supportive function. The impersonalization of life in urban culture has so conditioned man that he is no longer deeply moved by broken relationships, even those broken by death. Consequently community sorrow, insofar as it is expressed, is superficial and of no real value.

The major portion of *The American Funeral* is concerned with a study of the social-economic-psychological motivations of the participants in the modern funeral, that is, the funeral director and the mourning family (but not, interestingly enough, the pastor). The family seeks to utilize the funeral in a somewhat empty effort to gain social recognition and support. The funeral director seeks to assume more and more responsibility for the funeral, not merely for economic return but also to justify his broadening professional existence.

Bowman sets the context of his interpretation of the funeral by describing the six basic popular assumptions which he sees resting beneath the total structure of the present-day funeral.

(1) The sentiment of the bereaved centers, or should center, around the dead body; (2) the expenditure for the funeral, up to the utmost capacity of the family to pay, is the greatest criterion of the affection in which the dead was held; (3) the expenditure to be observed in the elegance of display at the funeral is a gauge of the status of the dead and the family in the community; (4)

the moral obligation rests on families to reveal their status through the style in which the funeral is conducted; (5) the beauty that is displayed at a funeral is a feature of the modern funeral. . . . (6) Apart from the religious aspects of funerals embodied in the rituals of certain faiths, a great social significance attaches to the disposal of the dead.[8]

The implicit manipulation suggested in these assumptions points up the tension which Bowman depicts as developing between the funeral participants—families and funeral directors.

The funeral director is seen as gradually increasing the areas of his influence and responsibility. His services are expanded, his counsel with regard to the form of the funeral is more widely sought, his subtle control of funeral practices is more firmly established. Bowman advances a number of reasons for this extension of the sphere of influence of the funeral director. Partly it is a matter of sheer efficiency. Since the majority of funeral services are provided by the funeral director, it is to his advantage to have them regulated so as to reduce wasted motion to afford maximum utilization of facilities. By standardizing his services he feels he can better serve his clients.

Another reason advanced for the tightening of control over the funeral by funeral directors is that of economic gain. Extension of funeral practices and services increases the cost of the funeral and the profit of the funeral industry. Bowman sees this as a manifestation of the economic pattern of our culture rather than as naked greed on the part of funeral directors. He also points out that the profit results from attitudes which pervade our culture; for example, that affection can be expressed through expenditure and that social status derives from conspicuous consumption.

Bowman also suggests that the funeral director's tendency

[8] *Ibid.*, pp. 100-101.

to increase control over the funeral is due to the lack of a specific body of knowledge in mortuary science. The struggle for professional recognition, which involves both social and economic status, assumes not only the capacity to render a service but also the possession of a considerable body of knowledge. It is this latter requirement that normally makes professional standing dependent upon extensive graduate education. Since such a body of knowledge is absent in mortuary science, or is almost totally a derivation from the professional fields of medicine and law or even theology, Bowman indicates that the funeral director seeks professional status only through his capacity to render service. Thus the more service he can render, the more he can be regarded as a professional.

It is also proposed that the aggressiveness of the funeral director in exercising control over the funeral is a reaction to the personal slights he has received, the lack of acceptance which he has been made to feel. Bowman offers some interesting reflections about the feelings of the bereaved toward the funeral director. He suggests that they view him with considerable ambivalence. On the one hand, they are very relieved that someone is capable of caring for the body of the deceased, since this would be extremely difficult for the mourners. On the other hand, their aversion to the body of the deceased and the guilt which this creates in them also cause them to project some hostility or resentment on the funeral director. An awareness of such unconscious resentment may cause the funeral director to try all the harder to serve in as many ways as possible or may lead him to a defensive rationalization of the costliness of the service he renders.

Bowman sees two major results arising from the funeral director's striving to increase the scope of his responsibility. One of these results is the growing emphasis on the body of the deceased. Since preparation of the body is the major area of service unique to the funeral director, most of the elaborations of the funeral will naturally be connected to this function. Embalming and cosmetology make possible public viewing of the body, as well as a longer time period between death and the final disposition of the body. Bowman regards this emphasis on the body as a hindrance to emotional adjustment and to the acceptance of reality. He also agrees with those who regard it as a limitation of spiritual values in an age of growing materialism.

The second result of the increasing influence of the funeral director is seen as the secularization of the funeral. Bowman is not blaming the funeral directors for secularism, but is saying that their widening function more and more reinforces the relegation of the church to the peripheral and the clergy to the superficial. Contemporary elaboration of the funeral is seen as weakening rather than strengthening the religious aspects of that service. Although Bowman can state that the funeral should provide security in terms of the sympathy of friends, the promises of religion, and thoughtful self-examination, he does not see much prospect for such help in the contemporary funeral.

The final portion of Bowman's study is a presentation of some possible new meanings for the funeral. Leadership (except the religious leadership of the clergy) needs to be transferred to influences that are social and professional. Technical and materialistic features need to be subordinate to psychological, social, and spiritual aspects. There should be less emphasis on the body. Plans should be formulated for sensible disposition. Costs and social obligations for the bereaved family need to be reduced. Collective action through burial societies should be used to reduce exploitation. Procedures following death should be geared to functioning communities. The funeral should be a part of an effort to develop maturity. Concern should be for enhancing life's values for the living.

There are several criticisms which might be made of Bowman's study. Certainly there is help to be found in the way in which he sees social phenomena related to the funeral. He acknowledges that many features of funeral practices are reflections of the culture, such as materialism, status seeking, evasion of reality. However, his contention that urbanization and industrialization have made the funeral an anachronism may be somewhat overstated. It certainly is regrettably true that these social factors may reduce the possibility of group support in bereavement. But there are many other values in the funeral that are not adversely affected by changing social settings. One wonders if the needs of a metropolitan bereaved family are so totally different from the needs of the bereaved in town and country that the funeral helps one and not the other. Is the funeral so remotely connected to common human needs that it is effective only in a particular kind of sociological setting?

This leads to another possible criticism. Is there not a certain limitation involved in utilizing the tools of only one social science? Man can be studied from the point of view of sociology, of psychology, of biology, or of theology. It is quite natural and legitimate that Bowman concentrate on the sociological, but there is always the danger that concentration upon one perspective may result in a deficiency in another dimension.

There are some helpful psychological observations in the book, but there are other instances where the psychological insights must be questioned. This stands out most obviously when the place of the body of the deceased in the mourning process is considered. At a number of points Bowman presents the value of speedy disposition of the body as a way of pointing to the reality of the loss, the finality of the breach of relationship, and the acceptance of separation. This is a valid point in some instances. However, fuller awareness of the dynamics often operative in the mourning situation will indicate the frequent possibility that speedy disposition actually represents an escape mechanism, a means for the evasion of reality and a getting rid of the body in an attempt to avoid the pain of full consideration of the separation. When the true complexity of some of the dynamics of mourning is taken into account, one finds that it is much more important to consider carefully the motivation for a particular act, such as speedy disposition of the body, rather than the act itself. This would mean that each individual situation has to be considered in itself, a step which is not easy in the broad social or economic point of view.

Nevertheless, *The American Funeral* represents a sizable forward step in the application of the methods of social science to the study of the funeral. It has some extremely fruitful observations to make. But its strength is also its weakness in that at times it does not take into sufficient account the complexity of the dynamics of individual situations.

A Satirical Critique

Nearly five years passed before the emergence of the next widely read popular critique of the funeral. Jessica Mitford captured the eyes of American readers with her humorous and satirical volume, *The American Way of Death*.

Mitford made little pretext of undertaking a serious social-scientific study. There is no apparent endeavor to deal comprehensively with the funeral in its social and psychological dimensions. The purpose of the author appears to have been to write a popular best-selling book, and she fulfilled that objective most successfully.

A secondary set of goals is also apparent. These cluster around the intention to simplify and rationalize the disposal of the dead. This would involve reducing the cost of the funeral by breaking the monopoly of the funeral industry. But even more basic appears the desire to do away with the funeral altogether. Sources, cited with approval by Mitford, convey this point of view: for example, "The medical profession in Great Britain . . . [are] doing all they can to reduce funeral service to little more than simple rubbish disposal." [9]

The methodology employed by Mitford consists largely of extensive reading in the publications and trade journals of the funeral industry, together with interviews with representatives of associations of funeral directors. Some truly devastating quotations are drawn from the professional literature. However, the serious student regrets very much that no sources are cited in standard bibliographic form, thus making it almost impossible to examine such statements in their original context. The style of her writing is highly readable. The satire is broad and biting. The wording is so emotionally loaded that any serious scientific intent is obviously foresworn.

Mitford's line of argument is double pronged. On the one hand, she vigorously attacks the funeral industry; on the other, she levels an attack against the funeral itself. Her assumption seems to be that the practices of the funeral industry and the funeral itself are inextricably linked. The funeral, in her thinking, is so completely the creation of the funeral industry that any endeavor to remove the excesses of control by the funeral directors will almost necessarily also remove the funeral. Mitford can seek to accomplish both removals with enthusiasm.

Her indictment of the funeral industry has three points: economic greed, manipulation of the individual mourner and of society, pseudoprofessionalism.

According to her point of view there is a kind of economic determinism operative in the funeral. This is not understood broadly in terms of the total national economic structure but in terms of economic manipulation by the funeral industry. Those who make their living through the funeral are so firmly in control of funeral practices that they can exert numerous pressures to assure maximum profit for themselves. Mitford points to a number of devices by which the cost of funerals and the profits of the funeral industry are kept at a high level.

[9] Jessica Mitford, *The American Way of Death* (New York: Simon and Schuster, 1963), p. 211.

She describes the attitude of the funeral director in cynical terms: "The seller of funeral service has, one gathers, a preconceived, stereotyped view of his customers. To him, the bereaved person who enters his establishment is a bundle of guilt feelings, a snob and a status seeker." [10] He plays upon these emotions and utilizes a variety of sales techniques to insure that the person will spend as much as possible for funeral services. The overcrowding of the funeral industry combines with the relatively high overhead costs to make it difficult for many funeral directors to maintain their businesses without an unreasonably high margin of profit, according to Mitford. Not only is the individual funeral director seen as the offender. The author goes on to demonstrate the way in which the profession as a whole has lobbied successfully to enact legal regulation of funeral practices and created a virtual monopoly. Any thoughtful and objective observer will admit that there is validity in many of the charges that are leveled. Yet in many instances one wonders at the breadth of the generalizations in which the indictments are stated.

Mitford sees the funeral industry engaged in a massive effort to manipulate both the individual mourner and the public by exercising firm control over funeral practices and by manufacturing new customs disguised as traditional practices of long standing. The purpose of such manipulation is regulation of the funeral to assure that profitable patterns will not be destroyed and to open the way for the extension of services to increase the profit. She proposes, within the limits of her norms, that the individual mourner should be free to express something of his need and to work out something of its satisfaction.

Mitford wages the third point in her offensive against the funeral industry by seeking to undercut the "professional stance" of the funeral director. She points to the nonprofes-

[10] *Ibid.*, p. 22.

sional status of the mortician in terms of the usual criteria for such status: graduate training, assembling of a broad body of knowledge unique to that discipline, and regulation by a comprehensive ethical standard of practice. Her contention is that the desire of the funeral director to achieve professional status is usually economically motivated, because usually the professional person is given the privilege of assessing the worth of his services rather than being subject to a standardized wage scale.

The second major phase of the attack is directed against the funeral itself. As in many of the other critiques the inference is strong that the funeral is no longer a valid experience and may as well be laid to rest itself.

At several points Mitford speaks of making a "rational" approach to the funeral. This approach is never fully defined, and we can learn what it is only by implication. It is quite possible to agree with her that the funeral must be rational as it seeks to assist the mourners to face and to accept the reality of their situation. It is equally possible to agree that the practicality which reason urges should be one of the norms of funeral practice. Reasonable dictates against waste, extravagance, excess are certainly valid. But an alternate understanding of rationality may well be what is intended by Mitford. It is possible to assume that she means funeral practice that is guided only by reason and is not in any sense geared to meeting emotional needs. The ideal rational man would thus appear to be above the stirrings of emotion. It is difficult to find this kind of bifurcation of man into reason and emotion meaningful. Or it may be that a rational approach to the funeral is synonymous with a humanistic approach which denies or disregards the dimension of man's life or his death that transcends the purely physical or mundane. This may be what Mitford has in mind when she lauds "those who would like to see an end to all the malarkey that surrounds the usual

74

kind of funeral." [11] The only meaningful references to the Christian position on death and burial are found in comments of Bishop James Pike.[12] His few brief statements deal quite properly with the desirability of avoiding ostentation, of respectful regard for the body of the deceased, of recognizing the propriety of holding the funeral in the church because it is a religious service.

There is a somewhat nostalgic tone in one aspect of Mitford's argument. She speaks with affection and longing about the good old days when friends of the family lovingly and simply cared for the dead without any "professional assistance." They washed and dressed the corpse, made a simple coffin, dug the grave in the churchyard. While there might be a certain attraction for the era which preceded the present division of labor, it is highly problematical whether it would be possible or desirable to return to it. In the present age a sick member of the family is cared for in the hospital rather than in the home, not because there is no love in the home, but because the hospital is better equipped and staffed for the task. In a day of maternity hospitals, nursing homes for the aged, textile mills, and manufacturing plants there will never be a return to childbirth at home, care in the family circle from cradle to grave, total family self-sufficiency as in bygone days. Is it less reasonable to assume that there will never be a return to the practice of friends laying out the body, making the coffin, digging the grave? We need to ask whether all this is the result of broad social change or the greedy scheming of medicine, business, and industry to intrude themselves upon man's freedom to be self-sufficient. Mitford's neglect of the social dimension leads her astray at this point.

Because she seems unable to divorce the funeral from her objections to the funeral industry, Mitford apparently feels

[11] *Ibid.*, p. 161.
[12] *Ibid.*, pp. 245 ff.

that the best solution is to do away with the funeral. By doing this she accepts the presuppositions of her opponents and defines the funeral in terms of the funeral industry—the very point to which she has objected so vehemently.

She gives no real attention to the alternate possibility of defining the funeral as a religious service, based on the place of the funeral in the ritual and tradition of Protestantism, Roman Catholicism, and Judaism. This dimension is almost totally absent in her writing. It would seem, then, that in her desire to object to the perversion of the meaning of the funeral, she has neglected her best possible resource: the original sources of the tradition in religion.

Nor does she give credence to the humanitarian possibilities of the funeral as a means for relieving in a therapeutic way the suffering of bereavement. Although Mitford repeatedly implies that psychiatric validation of the funeral would be normative, she shows almost total disregard for the psychological understanding of funeral practices. She gives no evidence of awareness of the work of Lindemann, Feifel, Eissler, and Farberow. She seems to be completely ignorant of the efforts of pastoral theology to deal with the subject. If one were to take her literally, it would seem that a psychological understanding of the funeral is only a devious gimmick used by a mortician to rationalize and sell his wares.

There is in this book a strong endorsement of memorial societies as a means for reducing funeral costs through cooperatives. The aim of such groups to provide services which are modest and dignified is commendable. A problem again begins to arise, however, when one finds in the statements of purpose of some such groups the desire to do away with the funeral. "The major objective of all the societies is to smooth the path for the family which prefers to hold a memorial service, without the body present, instead of the 'open casket' funeral." [13]

[13] *Ibid.*, p. 268.

It is not the right of a family to reach such a decision which is contestable, but the motive which may need examination. For some there may be no problem at all; for others there may be here a pattern of avoidance of painful reality that may make their mourning more difficult.

The contributions of the Mitford volume are several. In spite of her disavowal of the fact that our culture is involved in current funeral practices she offers, even though unintentionally, a stern and sharp commentary on the materialism of our age. She offers some constructive possibilities of implementing the desire for more economical funerals through memorial societies. She provides helpful referrals for those who desire to bequeath their bodies to tissue banks or medical schools. She points to some palpable situations involving exploitation and monopolization which require thoughtful attention.

However, in spite of these contributions there are some negative criticisms of this work. Foremost among these are superficiality, oversimplification, and bias. She sees the funeral almost solely in materialistic and economic terms. She denigrates sociological, psychological, and anthropological insights. She utilizes an extremely narrow cultural context for her argument, limiting it to the funeral industry rather than to the entire American social and economic structure. She longs for a return to the old ways in one narrow segment of life without any desire for a similar repristination of many other areas of living. She appears to encourage the tendency toward avoidance and evasion of reality which is all too common in our day. She does not see that reform of the funeral can take place without destruction of the funeral.

A Commonsense Critique

Another recent critical study of the funeral is *The High Cost of Dying*, by Ruth Mulvey Harmer, which is similar in purpose to Mitford, and yet more moderate in its tone. The goal seems to be reform or removal of the funeral. Her major thrusts are directed in three ways: reduction of the cost of the funeral, removal of the funeral from the control of the funeral directors, and the advocacy of memorial societies.

Harmer recognizes that the broad problems posed by present funeral practices can be met only through a comprehensive, sustained educational approach. This purpose is reflected in her style. Her writing is only mildly satirical. She makes no great effort to employ the methodology of the social or psychological sciences, offering instead a commonsense exposure of the situation and a persuasive presentation of remedies.

Harmer's position begins with a questioning of the meaningful nature of the funeral. Like other critics she is not convinced that the funeral can be a significant experience in our time. She has some insight into the purpose which the funeral is meant to fulfill.

It [the funeral] does provide during a period of crisis a set of customs or rituals that minimize the traumatic effect of the experience and offer other members of the group an opportunity for spiritual and secular communion. . . . Funerals can help to alleviate the pain of individuals affected by offering a series of actions that must be performed and by offering the solace that grief is shared by others.[14]

But Harmer contends that the modern funeral does very little to meet such needs and that it actually neutralizes such values. She feels that the funeral fails because it establishes a climate of unreality, because it is public in nature, and because it intensifies the shock. On this basis she reaches the conclusion that a new alternative for fittingly commemorating the dead can be found which will make the funeral unnecessary. This

[14] Ruth Mulvey Harmer, *The High Cost of Dying* (New York: Collier Books, 1963), p. 225.

alternative appears to be the small, private memorial service.

The reasons for the lack of proper meaning in the funeral and for the excessive cost are due to the operations of the funeral industry. "It has also exploited the worst of our motivations and desires: snobbery, vanity, the chance to rid ourselves of feelings of guilt through a pay off." [15] Harmer also objects to the economic structure of the funeral, citing the by now familiar facts of too many funeral homes for the available business, price fixing, and excessive unit cost.

Unlike Mitford, Harmer is willing to see that there is a connection between the funeral and the culture. "The American funeral—with its vulgarity, sacrifice of spiritual values to materialistic trappings, immature indulgence in primitive spectacles, unethical business practices, and overwhelming abnegation of rational attitudes—has become for many students of the national scene a symbol of cultural sickness." [16]

To this she adds what may be an even more potent factor from our cultural situation—the hunger for attention of the individual who has been thoroughly depersonalized by the busyness and loneliness of life. This may be seen in the desire of a person to have his own death memorialized in a way that hopefully will make some small mark, or the need for mourners to know that in suffering and sadness they may find a bit of the social support that is ordinarily lacking in life.

There are a number of proposals for changes in funeral practices offered in this volume. There is encouragement for establishing patterns to allow a more speedy disposition of the body of the deceased. It is proposed that immediate disposal, or at least within a day's time, would eliminate the need for embalming and would reduce the period of acute suffering.

A second proposal for change comes through support given

[15] *Ibid.*, p. 30.
[16] *Ibid.*, p. 13.

to memorial societies and funeral cooperatives. Such organizations are seen as offering a number of definite advantages. They enable the reduction of funeral costs because of the simplicity of their funeral services. They offer a channel for educating the public for possible revision of funeral practices by providing group support for variation from the cultural norm. They encourage a more rational and less emotional response to the funeral and its meaning. It is suggested that the universal need for some facilities to care for the body of the deceased and the wants of the mourners justifies consideration of regarding funeral arranging as a public utility. The purpose of any of these steps, according to the author, would be to offer to the individual family freedom either to plan a fully conventional funeral or to make plans in a way more suitable to their preference. It is indicated that most memorial societies advocate immediate cremation or a prompt private burial service. The reasons for this are seen as economy and the lessening of pain.

Closely related is another proposal, that of the substitution of the memorial service for the funeral. It is suggested that this enables the stripping away of pagan emphases on the material, the avoidance of extravagance, the obviation of embalming. It is the feeling that many of the more apparent difficulties present in the contemporary funeral would be avoided through more widespread adoption of memorial services.

Again we need to point out that the whole area of motivation must be considered in dealing with such proposals for change. It is quite possible that in merely seeking to avoid expense or emotional distress other kinds of distress may be brought about or the needs of the individuals may not be as fully met.

From a critical viewpoint it would appear that one of the major difficulties with the Harmer volume is the lack of thoughtful and precise definition. There are a number of points where this poses problems. The author fails to define the legitimate ways in which the funeral meets human need and therefore easily confuses them with aberrations that have developed. For example, "In the present system, the industry has on its side not only the laws it has helped to write, but our attitudes that it has remolded to conform to its own interests: respect for the dead, the need for ritualistic expressions of grief, the desire to conform to socially approved standards, the yearning for tangible evidence of immortality." [17] Granted, such attitudes are open to real question if the only reason for their existence is to necessitate elaborate funerals. But we need to ask: Are these not also in a very real sense ways in which the funeral through many centuries has properly sought to meet human need?

Harmer also argues that the contemporary funeral is a radical departure from the Judeo-Christian heritage. She sees that there is a possible correlation between religious belief and burial practice, a fact supported by both cultural anthropology and the history of religions. She does not deal specifically with the religious elements of the funeral. In fact, at times this lack of more substantial treatment of the religious aspects of the funeral creates some problems. For example, there is the implication that there is great similarity between the view of death held by Socrates and the Judeo-Christian tradition, showing no awareness of the fundamental distinction between Greek dualism and the Judeo-Christian unitary concept of man's being.

Harmer joins other critics of the funeral in explicating a desire to give up the funeral. "Indeed, the question of whether or not any funeral can be meaningful is one that must be given serious consideration if our belief in human values is to be preserved." [18] Such a position would imply that funerals are such empty, synthetic forms that they cannot possibly be of value. No truly serious attempt is made to understand and present either the psychological or the theological

[17] *Ibid.*, p. 30.
[18] *Ibid.*, p. 224.

rationale for the funeral. There is truth in the charge that some funerals lack meaning, but it is oversimplification to assert that therefore all funerals lack meaning. Harmer misses the fact that there can be a qualitative difference in funerals.

Another somewhat distressing note is the emphasis on privacy which one finds in the normative views presented by Harmer. There is repeated suggestion that the experiences of death, bereavement, and the funeral should be kept within the confines of the primary social group, i.e., the immediate family. The community dimension of these experiences is not given much attention. This may be due to agreement with Bowman's thesis that the bigness of society has virtually destroyed meaningful community beyond the family circle. But if community is becoming so unreal, is it not questionable that one should foster the abolition or neglect of a social and religious resource for embodying meaningful community in one of the universal crisis experiences of life?

Limitation and Value in the Critiques

These four volumes represent major critiques of the funeral widely read in this generation. Numerous articles and reports could be added to this list, but these contain basically the same positions. Having examined in detail the purposes and lines of argument of these authors, we would seek now to summarize the limitations and values of these analyses.

One of the most outstanding limitations of the critiques is the narrow focus upon the economic aspects of the problem. Without exception the authors have devoted themselves to protesting the high cost of the funeral. Too often the implication is that cost is really all that matters. While one would not deny that there is validity in the concern for cost, there are other dimensions which need to be included as well. Extravagance is certainly questionable. But if other values of the funeral, values of a social, psychological, and religious nature are considered, the whole subject of cost may be seen in a different perspective. By failing to give credence to the possibility of any values other than the sheer material trappings of the funeral and their costliness, the critics seem to yield to the very materialism which they so vociferously decry. In the very nature of their protest they forcefully make the very point they are seeking to resist. Consequently they end up locked in a competitive struggle with the funeral interests for the consumer's dollar.

A second limitation, which grows out of the first, involves the danger of discarding what is of value in an effort to remove what is faulty. For the most part the critiques appear to assume that the only alternatives are either to maintain the status quo in funeral practice or to do away with the funeral altogether because its development has not been totally satisfactory. This is a questionable assumption, especially when the only facet of the funeral which has been considered with any thoroughness is the economic. It is not a foregone conclusion that the value of the funeral has been irreparably destroyed by the commercial interests related to funeral practice. It is possible to demonstrate that there are elements of the funeral which have brought value to individuals for many centuries. It can be shown that, even though some of these values may have been obscured by elaborations of the funeral patterns, the values persist and can be restored to full effectiveness.

A third limitation is found in the lack of objectivity which is too often found in the critiques. One gauge of this is the way in which pejorative terms are used. Sometimes this is relatively harmless, even amusing. But from the standpoint of scholarship such word usage—for example, the various terms applied in derision to funeral directors—detracts from the serious purpose of the study. Still more significant is the facile use of such a term as "pagan" without any precise definition. Paganism can be used as a label of disapproval, a brand of odium, like communism. Or it can be used to point objectively to that which has its origins in primitive society outside the Judeo-Christian tradition. Or with further refinement it can be objectively applied to that which has presuppositions that contradict the Judeo-Christian position. The first usage is unacceptable because it is completely lacking in definition. The second and third are acceptable and useful so long as they are interpreted carefully. The Judeo-Christian view does not reject something as pagan because it had its origins in pagan culture. For instance, among those things which would have to be rejected if this were the case would be some of the great myths found in the Old Testament, portions of the legal code of the Scriptures, our calendar, numerous holidays and festivals. The criterion which has traditionally been applied is: Can an alien custom be given Judeo-Christian meaning or does a custom originating outside the tradition stand in basic contradiction to Judeo-Christian principles? If this kind of stringent definition is applied, it should be carefully noted that pagan funeral practices include such things as avoidance of the reality of death, total disregard for the body as well as total attention to the body, and assumptions about immortality of the soul. These things are contradictions of the Judeo-Christian heritage and are legitimately regarded as pagan. Rarely is the term used with precision. Absence of definition or the emotional loading of words constitute loss of objectivity, and thus become a limitation of the critiques.

There are, however, a number of positive contributions which emerge from the critical analyses of the funeral. Either directly or indirectly all of them provide a diagnostic picture of the failings of contemporary culture. Some of the authors are prepared to state these facts openly as observed data; others may deny them overtly but manifest them covertly in their own form and content. The cultural phenomena which figure most largely in the studies are materialism, status seeking, conformity, manipulation, and escapism. These are the marks of our age which also have their effect on the funeral. The studies, insofar as they are willing to deal with the culture itself, offer real value in assisting our understanding of some of the broad cultural problems which confront us and our efforts to work toward their solution.

A second major positive contribution of the critiques is the impetus they provide for an examination of funeral interests. Certainly this need not be construed as a vendetta against funeral directors, cemetery managements, and manufacturers of funeral goods. Yet there is no reason to assume a kind of sanctity surrounding funeral interests which would question the validity of any scrutiny of the funeral as a cultural, religious, or business phenomenon.

Any critical study should not involve special pleading either for or against funeral interests. It should be as objective as possible. Its methodology should be grounded in principles of sound research established by the social sciences, psychology, and theology.

The funeral cannot be studied in isolation. It must be understood in the context of the total economic system in which it exists, a system that involves competition between business establishments, manipulation of the customer by advertising and motivational research, techniques for promoting maximum sales, and appeals to conspicuous consumption. Present-day studies are valid only insofar as they deal with the funeral in this larger sense.

Modern critiques consistently make several charges against funeral interests. There is the claim that the funeral is controlled by monopolistic practices. Evidence includes such things as the expulsion by associations of funeral directors of members who have entered into contracts with burial cooperatives, or the insistence of crematories that a casket be incinerated with the body. Practices of this order require careful scrutiny by responsible regulatory agencies.

Another charge involves economic exploitation by funeral

directors. This does not refer merely to the infrequent instances of high-pressure selling which are reported. More commonly observed is the single pricing method generally used, offering only a total price rather than a list of services and their costs from which the bereaved family might make a selection. In this way very few options are available. Or one could cite the appeals which are sometimes made to status or to the sense of obligation to the deceased, or one might point to the way in which advertising and display are used to manipulate the purchaser. But, as we have indicated, these are also parts of the standard business practice of our time. This makes them no less regrettable. Still, it becomes apparent that the funeral is no freer from monopoly and exploitation within the bounds of legality than are the majority of commercial interests in our society. So a critique of economic practices surrounding the funeral must involve a broader criticism of the business practices generally found in our time.

A third charge offered by funeral critics is that the preference of the individual is thoroughly regulated by contemporary funeral practices. This is seen in a number of ways. There is the standardization of components of the funeral. The funeral is regarded as a comprehensive structure. Little encouragement is given by the funeral interests to individual innovation. The way in which arrangements are made, according to an established schedule of features, assumes a considerable measure of conformity on the part of the bereaved. It should be pointed out that there is both advantage and disadvantage in this. A degree of stability is very helpful to mourners shaken by the trauma of their grief. To have an established structure of funeral practices is valuable to them. But at the same time to hold this structure too rigidly does not allow the funeral to be responsive to their individual needs. Of course it is wrong for a family to be coerced into arranging an elaborate funeral for which they feel no need. It seems equally wrong for them to be coerced to arrange an austere disposition of the body when they need the support of the more traditional funeral pattern. Manipulative salesmanship in any field has a certain repugnance for anyone who cherishes his freedom of choice. It would appear, then, that a bereaved family should be free to choose the kind of funeral service which they feel will be most helpful to them in their particular need. Ideally, the funeral will involve both structure and flexibility. All those who are involved—funeral director, pastor, mourners—need to seek to maintain this balance.

The last of the positive points growing out of the critical studies of the funeral is this: we see here the pressing need for adequate, broadly based, objective criteria for assessing the validity of the funeral. As has been pointed out, many of the critiques are lacking in objectivity. In some instances the emotional bias of the author was all too evident. Virtually all of the studies have used economy as the major objective norm for their considerations. As we have indicated, this norm, while valid, is not sufficient by itself for judging the funeral. It becomes increasingly necessary that we should draw together a number of disciplines in developing criteria by which to evaluate the effectiveness of the funeral. The insightful judgments of cultural anthropology, psychology, social psychology, and theology need to be added to the norm of economy.

The critical studies of the funeral have been greeted by some with real enthusiasm as forthright statements designed to expose and correct grievous wrongs in modern funeral practice. Others have viewed the studies with alarm, as if sacred cows were about to be slaughtered. We need to examine the critiques carefully, seeking to assess their claims with fairness and objectivity, pointing to their weaknesses and limited perspectives. We need to find stimulation from them for making more careful and profound assessment of values which can be found in the funeral and means for conserving them.

Unanswered Questions

Against this background I would enumerate several questions that remain to be answered. The solution of these problems constitutes the task to which the serious student of the funeral devotes himself.

1. What is the value of the funeral? Almost every critic, even the most satirical, implies that once the funeral had values which it no longer possesses. These values, either in the past or the present, need definition and delineation.

2. How is it possible to conserve the values of the funeral? Assuming that values are found to exist or to have existed in the funeral, some steps need to be taken to retain or restore them in their rightful places. The funeral should not then be too easily written off as an effective social and religious resource for the bereaved.

3. What constitutes objectivity in assessing the funeral? This question takes into account that the dynamics operative in the person of the critic or the advocate become involved in the evaluation. The reaction of persons to the basic fact of death, emotional response to the body of the deceased, and personal involvement in the experience of bereavement may well make objectivity extremely difficult. One needs to be very much aware of the complexity of the question.

4. What are the most comprehensive criteria for determining what is of value in the funeral and what is not of value? Very few who have given any thought to the funeral would suggest that everything should remain just as it is. But sound, objective bases need to be established for the determination of value. Subjective opinion, bias based on personal experience, or special pleading do not constitute effective means for such evaluation.

What then is the funeral?

88

5

Dimensions of
Definition

The funeral is multidimensional and thus requires a multidimensional definition. This is the point that has so often been missed. Most of the fields of human knowledge have recognized that simple, precise definition is extremely difficult, if not impossible, in many realms. A definition tends to lack meaning and ultimately usefulness if the perspective of the definer is not taken into account. This is not to say that the one who offers the definition is necessarily biased or deceptive or intellectually dishonest. It is to say that definition is always made from a given perspective.

It follows that a specific object may be defined legitimately from a number of perspectives. Even the fact that these perspectival definitions are not congruent does not destroy their value. Rather it enlarges and enriches our knowledge of the object being defined.

James Knight has written: "It is the misfortune of our time that we expend great effort attacking our traditions and ceremonials without understanding their usefulness to men through the ages." [1] Part of this misfortune is due to the fact that careful definition has not been undertaken; that only very limited perspectives have been employed; that one perspectival definition has been used to cancel out, rather than to supplement, another.

[1] Introduction to Edgar N. Jackson's *For the Living* (Des Moines: Channel Press, 1964), p. 11.

89

Our task, then, is not the elaboration of many definitions of the funeral, but to explore several varying dimensions of a definition. It is not a matter of determining which definitions are more adequate or more to our liking. Our effort is to enrich our understanding of the funeral by exploring several of its dimensions and the accompanying perspectival definitions.

We should acknowledge that the funeral is dealt with here in optimum terms: what it can be and ought to be. This is done in full recognition that the contemporary funeral is not always understood or carried out in its best form and intention.

Four of the perspectives from which the funeral may be considered are the cultural anthropological, social psychological, psychological, and theological. In each of these dimensions we shall find elements of definition to enlarge and deepen our understanding of the funeral.

The Perspective of Cultural Anthropology

As a discipline anthropology has been interested in funeral practices of a given culture as effective means for deepening understanding of a people and their conception of existence. The work of Malinowski, Benedict, Mead, and many others has acknowledged that the customs surrounding death and bereavement are integral parts of a given cultural pattern. In the great preponderance of cultures which have been investigated in detail there has been some ritual means for denoting the ending of a life and for indicating an understanding of a new existence in some form, however primitive it might seem.

Malinowski has hypothesized that primitive man is first moved to religious activity by his confrontation of the mysterious power of death.[2] Faced with this force which he takes to

[2] Bronislaw Malinowski, "The Art of Magic and the Power of Faith," *Theories of Society*, ed. by Talcott Parsons (New York: Free Press, 1961), II, 1189-91.

be hostile, man strives to defend himself against it by attempting to control it. This he tries to accomplish by controlling the events which surround death. According to this theory various burial rituals had their original impetus in fear, perhaps accompanied by a sense of awe. Thus it would be assumed that ritual developed almost compulsively from random behavior because of the necessity to control the fearful forces surrounding death.

In a slightly different vein Mandelbaum points to the apparent necessity for every group to develop some plan of action for coping with the event of death. He points out that even though a given individual may be confused or unprepared for the reality of death, the social group almost always can provide guidance and support for him because it possesses a relatively stable pattern of behavior for meeting the crisis. Mandelbaum writes:

Certain things must be done after a death, whether it occurs in a very simple or in a highly complex society. The corpse must be disposed of; those who are bereaved—who are personally shocked and socially disoriented—must be helped to reorient themselves; the whole group must have a known way of readjustment after the loss of one of its members. These things "must" be done in the sense that they are done. When people find that they have no set pattern for dealing with death—as may occur in newly coalesced groups—or when they discover that the former pattern is no longer a feasible one, they tend quickly to establish some clear plan for coping with the occasion of death.[3]

In this explanation we find an elaboration of the coping function, moving beyond the fear of death to efforts to maintain meaningful life for those who survive. Thus the group seeks to cope not only with the mysterious power of death but

[3] David G. Mandelbaum, "Social Uses of Funeral Rites," *The Meaning of Death*, ed. by Herman Feifel (New York: McGraw-Hill Book Company, 1959), p. 189.

with the actual hurt which death has caused for individuals and for the group.

Another aspect of the meaning of the funeral seen through anthropological studies relates the functions that were directed toward the deceased rather than the bereaved. One of the very helpful tools for understanding this stratum of funeral practices in many cultures is a pattern described by van Gennep as *rite de passage*.[4] Extensive cross cultural studies indicated to him that there were observable common patterns in ceremonies that accompanied some of the crucial experiences of human individual and social life—birth, adolescence, marriage, death. The rituals signified a passage from one important state of being to another. Van Gennep saw these rites as having three major phases which he described as separation from a former state, transition to a new state, and incorporation into that new state.

Although he did a great deal to demonstrate the wide existence of these patterns, he cautioned on several occasions that he was not claiming absolute universality nor absolute necessity for these ritual patterns. He pointed out that the funeral ceremonies particularly may be somewhat less typical of the pattern because they may be influenced by religious beliefs about life after death, or may be ritual means for guarding the living from the hostility of the spirit of the dead, or may be ceremonial ways for purifying those who have had direct contact with the dead. Such elements in funeral practice are undoubtedly present in many instances, but the wide usage that is still made of van Gennep's model after half a century would appear to indicate that later scholars feel that it is a valid position for interpreting at least part of the function of the funeral.

The fact that death brings separation is so obvious that it

[4] Arnold van Gennep, *The Rites of Passage*, trans. by Monika Vizedom and Gabrielle Caffee (Chicago: University of Chicago Press, 1960). Originally published in French in 1908.

is reasonable to assume that funeral customs would invariably convey this aspect of the experience. Actually and symbolically there is indication that the deceased is separated from the life that he has lived and from the living. As van Gennep indicates[5] there are numerous elements in funeral practice that typify separation. Included here would be the custom in some primitive societies of destroying the property of the deceased, killing members of his immediate family or his household, regarding the deceased as taboo and therefore outside the circle of relationship. More contemporary practices, such as the destruction of the body by cremation or placing the body in a grave and the accumulation of graves in special burial grounds set apart for that purpose, represent elements of the process of separation of the dead from the living which is a part of funeral practice.

Very often it has been assumed that rites of separation are the only, or at least the major, theme of funeral practices. Van Gennep found that rites of transition are also extremely important. In a way, the time that is taken up by various funeral practices becomes a time of transition, transition from the state of living to the state of death. There are some practices, such as the efforts for preservation of the body, the display of the body, rituals involving the dissolution of the body, the formal period of mourning, which can be understood as efforts to maintain a diminishing relationship with the deceased. Gradually the person is eased from the land of the living to the abode of the dead. In some cultures this transitional period seems to be characterized by a dual assumption: that a diminishing relationship can be maintained with the dead (most often involving the corpse of the deceased) and that this transitional relationship is temporary, normally with a ritually defined terminus.

The third phase which can be observed in funeral practices

[5] *Ibid.*, pp. 164 ff.

is rites of incorporation. This can be seen as incorporating the deceased into a new state of existence, a life after death. Van Gennep, Frazer, and others have observed striking similarity between funeral rituals and certain initiatory rites. In the puberty rites of many cultures there are symbolic acts that indicate the "death" of the person as a child and the incorporation into the "new life" of the adult world. Many of the forms which are used in such initiations are also to be found in the funerary rituals of the people, indicating that the same pattern is being followed. In both circumstances the individual is incorporated into a new state and a new quality of relationship.

Although the van Gennep model also depicts the experience of the mourners in their separation from society by the traumatic loss of a loved one, in their transition to a way of life without the presence of the deceased, and in their reincorporation into the group in their changed state, we should take note here of the way in which these three phases of the rites of passage are applied in a very real sense to the deceased. We have here an indication that the focus on the needs of the mourners and the focus on the deceased are inextricably related. The one without the other lacks completeness and full meaning.

Lest we assume that such findings are possible only in simple, primitive cultures, we can look with profit at a study of a modern American city with its complex culture. Warner[6] has undertaken an examination of the meanings which shape the understandings of existence for citizens of a northeastern American city. Acknowledging that the funeral is a significant experience in the lives of these people, he probes it as a symbolic context for these meanings.

Warner asserts that all of man's social experience possesses

[6] W. Lloyd Warner, The Living and the Dead (New Haven: Yale University Press, 1959).

94

a rich content of symbols which portray the ways in which the group conceives the nature of man, the nature of the world and of that which is regarded as supernatural. These symbols may be fairly apparent and close to the surface, or they may be deeply buried in the social structure. The symbols not only have an influence upon the values and beliefs of the group, but these beliefs also influence formation and endurance of the symbols.

It is Warner's thesis that in funeral practices we can see certain values which consciously or unconsciously are being conserved or sought by the group. The major values which are symbolized in the funeral emerge in Warner's definition: "The funeral or *rite de passage* . . . symbolically translates the body from the world of the living to that of the dead and helps to reestablish the relations of living members of the group to each other and to the memory of the dead." [7]

He further observes that in the community death occurs with regularity and that the virtually unending repetition of funerals gives the members of the community renewed opportunities for ritual connection with the dead. In other words, the individual funeral is not the only focus. Similar functions are served by the cumulative experience of funerals in the community.

The funeral is a way in which the society provides symbols which can express the feelings of the mourners. It is not merely the private experience of these feelings that is important. The funeral customs of a community permit the public expression of feelings which need to be released by the bereaved. Very often we assume that this kind of release is applicable solely to the mourners most intimately related to the deceased. Warner's work suggests that there is much more involvement beyond this immediate circle of relationship than we sometimes assume. A funeral, as a public community rite, touches

[7] *Ibid.*, pp. 31-32.

every participant at the point of his own feelings toward death and toward the dead of his own relationship.

There is in the funeral, as well as in the more informal behavior that surrounds the funeral, the opportunity for the symbolic expression of both negative and positive feelings. The painful feelings which grow out of separation, the affection and appreciation in which the deceased was held, the personal fears of death, aggressive impulses or hostile feelings directed toward the deceased, and guilt can invest the symbols which are a part of the funeral customs and thus find release.

Although the anthropologist legitimately maintains his objectivity as a social scientist, he makes some observations about the religious functions of funeral customs. It is notable that according to the anthropologist, most often the religious function of the funeral is applied to the deceased rather than to the bereaved. Warner introduces the concept of the transition technician.

Although at such [crisis] times family members are very active, professional men are called in to take charge. . . . They are the transition technicians standing by as the time conveyor belt transports and transforms those who compose its traffic. They manipulate the highly valued symbols and play their part in defining and establishing what is happening to the lifetime of each individual and what this means in the social time of the groups.[8]

In the contemporary funeral Warner would see the minister and the funeral director as transition technicians. (It should be pointed out that this term is applied objectively and with no pejorative intent.) Their function is to facilitate the transition of the deceased from the state of living. Symbolic words and acts enable the mourners and the social group to reorient their relationship with the deceased from that of ordinary human interpersonal relatedness to a new state of relationship

[8] *Ibid.*, p. 306.

with one who is now part of a new dimension of existence. The funeral symbolically marks the removal of the deceased from the common humanity of which he has been a part and the entrance into an existence which is no longer subject to change and time.

The consideration of the funeral by anthropologists sees the rites as focusing on the dead as well as the living. This may be a fruitful insight for our consideration. Much of the emphasis of the Protestant funeral has been quite the opposite. It has been assumed that the funeral had only to do with the living.

Protestant theology has traditionally held that intercession is not made for the dead, that we cannot do anything to change or improve the status of those who have died. Thus masses for the dead and concepts of purgation have not been part of Protestant belief or practice. But the Protestant funeral in its best form rightly should not disregard the deceased. Certainly there is testimony to the fact that separation from life has occurred and that the deceased is becoming a part of a new phase of existence. Understood in symbolic terms the funeral becomes the way in which a community conveys its values and beliefs regarding the meaning of life and death, as well as its understanding of the transition of the deceased to a new existence.

The Perspective of Social Psychology

Very closely related to the preceding is the dimension of the funeral which is understood by social psychology. We will focus here on the funeral's value for the individual in the context of the group of which he is a part.

The funeral has a place in the process by which the mourner restructures his relationship with the deceased. This involves recognition of a change in both the deceased and the mourner. The deceased has changed because he has died and is no longer

97

a part of this aspect of existence which we call life. The mourner has changed because his life is now lived without the relationship to the deceased as he has known it. From the social psychological point of view the new relationship is largely one of recollection, memory, and the residue of past experience. The mourning process involves this relational transition.

The funeral also has social psychological meaning when we see it as part of the pattern through which the mourners interact with the society of which they are a part. There is something intensely personal in suffering. It is quite understandable that it produces a sense of isolation from the group. As it were, the suffering individual concentrates all of his personal energy, even that which is normally devoted to social participation, for meeting the crisis. The capacity for initiating or simply maintaining relationships is severely reduced. It is not uncommon for the bereaved to feel terribly alone in his sorrow.

Then follows a period of transition in which life is reorganized without the deceased. When this transition has been made, there is a reunion or reincorporation of the mourner into normal social relationships with the group. This process was much more apparent in a time when there were formal periods of mourning, distinctive mourning dress, standardized behavior that indicated bereavement. That pattern also involved a clearly defined time for the lifting of mourning.

Modern American social practices no longer follow such a pattern. In fact, where once there may have been a year of formal mourning, now the formally structured period is measured in days. Within a day or two following the funeral individuals are back at work, routines are reestablished, and behavior unique to mourning is abandoned. This means that the brief period, in which the funeral is one of the major focuses, is extremely important because it contains a condensation of the experiences which were formerly prolonged. If one views mourning merely as a painful, abnormal experience, this brevity is cause for rejoicing. If one sees mourning as a therapeutic process which inevitably requires time, there is concern that the brief period allotted be utilized with maximum effectiveness. A part of the vital function of the funeral is to assist in all three phases of the mourners' rite of passage during these days: the separation or isolation, the transition to life without the deceased, and reunion with the group.

The funeral can be understood as a ritual involving activity on the part of a social group. As a religious rite it binds the individual mourner and the group which shares his loss to the dimension of the sacred. But it also serves to bind the individual to the group. There is here an indication of the willingness of the group to share the suffering of loss insofar as this is possible. There is the willingness of the group to accept the mourner with all of his feelings. There is indication that the group stands ready to receive the bereaved back into relationship as soon as he is ready for such reunion. Group participation, indicating group solidarity, is a source of support and strength for the mourner.

Mandelbaum described this theme very well.

Rites performed for the dead generally have important effects for the living. A funeral ceremony is personal in its focus and is societal in its consequences. The people of every society have a pattern for dealing with the death of their fellows. No matter how unprepared an individual may be for the fact of a particular death, the group must always have some plan of action in the event of death.[9]

These are not just random activities. In the ritual the social group seeks to convey its understanding of the experiences which are taking place at the time of death and bereavement. It seeks to lift up the values which it desires to preserve. It

[9] David G. Mandelbaum, "Social Uses of Funeral Rites," p. 189.

seeks to point to those meanings which it believes will endure the onslaught of the crisis of death.

The funeral is a ritual which symbolizes the relative indestructibility of the group in the face of death. There is full recognition of the fact that a member of the group has died. However, even though the value of the past relationship with the deceased is no longer present, the group has survived. It is changed because of death, but it still exists as a meaningful entity.

The Perspective of Psychology

A third dimension of the funeral which will contribute to our understanding is the psychological. Although it is virtually impossible to consider the individual apart from the group for purposes other than discussion, this element of our study is devoted almost entirely to the mourner. Loss which comes through the death of one who has been part of a circle of relationship produces within the mourners psychological needs which can be met in the funeral. This was the thesis of an earlier book [10] and will not be dealt with here in exhaustive detail.

Eric Lindemann, who pioneered the modern psychiatric understanding of grief, wrote:

The funeral service is psychologically necessary in order to give the opportunity for "grief work." The bereaved must be given the capacity to work through his grief if he is to come out of that situation emotionally sound. Finally we need to see to it that those whom we serve are left with comforting memories. Some will argue this point. I think, however, it is sound psychologically.[11]

The assumption here is that the funeral is an integral part of the series of experiences through which a person passes in

[10] Paul Irion, *The Funeral and the Mourners.*
[11] Cited by Edgar N. Jackson, *For the Living,* p. 91.

the course of bereavement. Properly understood and carried out, it is not irrelevant to his deepest concerns in this crisis nor is it isolated from his most profound feelings.

The funeral is helpful psychologically insofar as it enables mourners to confront realistically the crisis in which they exist. As has been indicated in our earlier discussion, there is some basis for assuming that one of the points of origin for the funeral was the necessity to cope with the reality of death. It is quite obvious that such a coping function would be grievously hindered if the individual were unwilling or unable to face the fact that death has really occurred. Death is not an illusion that may be easily dismissed or evaded.

The person who accepts as reality that death has taken place is aided because there is then a reasonable explanation for the profound feelings which sweep over him in bereavement. He knows why life seems so empty, why he seems to be resentful of other people whose lives are untouched, why he wants to pull away from contact with others. In addition the individual is motivated to begin the painful process of mourning, the process of reorganizing life without the presence of the deceased.

The funeral underscores the reality of the bereavement situation as it offers realistic interpretation of what has taken place. It provides a kind of consensual validation because the mourner is joined by others in the group who are experiencing something of the same loss. The separation from the body of the deceased by burial or cremation further affirms that the relationship as it has been known has really been broken.

Acceptance of reality demands a response, which is seen in the various feelings evoked by bereavement in the mourners. Grief is often more than just sorrow for loss. There are some persons who are shaken by a variety of fears of the bleakness of existence without the loved one who has died or fears produced by reflection upon the possibility of their own death. Some may be troubled by feelings of hostility toward the de-

101

ceased, recalling the strained circumstances of relationship in the past. Others may be resentful because they feel so utterly abandoned and helpless. Some mourners will be distressed by guilt because of real or imagined wrongs they have done to the deceased or because of unresolved negative feelings harbored against him. It is not uncommon for mourners to be overwhelmed by disillusionment because the relationship that has given meaning to life is broken. Or it may be that the feelings of the bereaved are positive—gratitude and love. Each individual response is unique, but all have in common the need for expression.

Psychologically understood, this expression of the feelings of the bereaved serves a variety of purposes. It is a healthful catharsis giving release to pent-up feelings, making available for more constructive use energy which has been devoted to denying or avoiding such strong feelings. It is recognized that the emotional components accompanying bereavement can be repressed, delaying their expression for a considerable time. Ultimately, if the loss is to be truly assimilated, these feelings must be brought into the open and dealt with.

The need for catharsis is closely related to the need for developing insight. While catharsis is helpful, its healing capacity is limited without a growing awareness of the nature of the feelings that are released and some understanding of their origin. Although the funeral itself will very probably not be an occasion for insight, it can be an event in which catharsis is enabled, opening the way for the development of insight.

Another psychological function of the funeral is making possible a recollection of the deceased. Freud's early discussion of mourning begins to illuminate this task.

Reality passes its verdict—that the object no longer exists—upon each single one of the memories and hopes through which the libido was attached to the lost object, and the ego, confronted as it were with the decision whether it will share this fate, is persuaded by the sum of its narcissistic satisfactions in being alive to sever its attachment to the nonexistent object.[12]

Building on this foundation Lindemann's research has pointed to the necessity of "learning to live with memories of the deceased." [13] This is a matter of delicate balance. It would not be healthful for the mourner to try to recall the deceased from the dead by his memories, trying neurotically to perpetuate the relationship through illusion. Neither would it be healthful to seek to extinguish all memory of the deceased because of the painfulness of such recall. The deceased must be remembered in a context of finality as one who has lived and died. The remembrances help to maintain a relationship which is not radically ended but radically changed. In time the mourner becomes able to think of his relationship to the deceased, in both its positive and negative aspects, without pain. The funeral is of important help here because it can reinforce both the remembering process and the fact that the one who is remembered has died.

We must be reminded that not all of the psychological needs of mourners are conscious needs. Very often there are deeply ambivalent feelings of love and hostility, acceptance and rejection, which have been present in the relationship to the deceased. Death may serve to sharpen those feelings while at the same time causing greater repression of the negative pole of the ambivalence. Death may cause the mourner, for example, unconsciously to feel more deeply resentful toward the deceased. Yet consciously he is led by custom and the taboo against thinking ill of the dead to lay sole emphasis upon his positive feelings toward the deceased. The negativity is pushed into the unconscious to work its corrosive damage.

[12] Sigmund Freud, "Mourning and Melancholia," *Collected Papers*, IV, 166.
[13] Erich Lindemann, "Symptomatology and Management of Acute Grief," *American Journal of Psychiatry*.

The funeral in its public acceptance of the right of the mourner to express his authentic conscious feelings can afford a climate in which he ultimately may be free to express and assimilate all of his feelings.

The funeral itself is only part, sometimes even a small part, in the whole psychological process of meeting bereavement. Yet, because of its public nature, it is an extremely important part. It represents the response of the community or of the church to the emotional experiences of the mourner. Thus it cannot be regarded as either irrelevant or contradictory to the psychological processes of acceptance, release, expression, and assimilation that enable the mourner to endure and overcome the tremendous disorganization of his life which has taken place.

The Perspective of Theology

Finally we turn to the theological dimension. Funeral practices have been from the earliest times religious in nature. The investigations of cultural anthropology have been able to follow the course of development of a cult of the dead from early, even prehistoric times. "Since of all the mysterious, disintegrating and critical situations with which man has been confronted throughout the ages death appears to have been the most disturbing and devastating, it is hardly surprising that the earliest traces of religious belief and practice should center in the cult of the dead." [14] Studies of intentional interments from as early as the Middle Paleolithic age show the emergence of particular patterns for ceremonial treatment of the dead.

According to archaeological investigation it would appear that practices followed in development of the cult of the dead had as their major function provision of a way for dealing with

[14] E. O. James, *Prehistoric Religion* (London: Thames and Hudson, 1957), p. 17.

the mystery of death. Efforts were made to provide for the well-being of the one who had died and to sustain the survivors in their fear and awe as they faced death.

James advances the hypothesis that "when modes of burial begin to be stereotyped by tradition they may tend to influence beliefs about the locality and nature of the next life." [15] This hypothesis would affirm that primitive man recognized the radical dislocation created by death. He was unable to penetrate the mystery of this event, but he did seek ways to deal with it and with his own fear of it. As these coping rituals assumed more stable form and structure they became the basis for more abstract notions of what death was and what happened to the individual in death. Man's emotional needs in the face of the crisis created by death, according to James's hypothesis, produced ritualistic satisfaction which in turn produced abstract ideas and beliefs about the nature of life and death.

James, as an anthropologist, does not really need to be concerned with the question of whether this process is founded on objective reality or whether it is totally subjective. From his point of view this is not really an important issue. But for the one who seeks to approach the funeral theologically the question is crucial. The theological perspective will not deny the validity nor the importance of subjective experience. However, at the same time it will not assume that the answer which has been found is merely the product of man's striving or reflection but will affirm that it is founded upon objective reality. Even the fact that empirical validations cannot be given to this reality does not necessarily indicate that it is totally subjective in nature.

Although we have no desire to baptize the status quo as automatically Christian, it does seem evident that in the main the American understanding of the funeral has been religious.

[15] *Ibid.*, p. 133.

At least in principle, if not always in practice, the major emphases of the funeral have represented the Judeo-Christian heritage of the majority of the American population.

By this we mean that the formal intention and content of the American funeral service, regarded in optimum terms, represents a view of death, of the body of the deceased, of the resources available for meeting the needs of the mourners which is consonant with the understanding of life and death in Christian theology. Certainly it would be ridiculous to assert that the modern funeral in actual practice is totally in harmony with the understanding of Christian theology. There are numerous practices in vogue today which obviously do not meet that criterion. However, this does not mean that the funeral itself cannot be defined theologically.

We should note here again that the perspective from which we view the funeral will be that of Protestant Christian theology. We cannot presume to speak from the viewpoint of Judaism or Roman Catholicism. This delineation represents no judgment on other points of view but is a deliberate narrowing of the scope to enable more intensive treatment.

Speaking now of the funeral in terms of its best form and usage, let us see how it represents adequately this theological position. The funeral, thus considered, does bear witness to an understanding of death which sees this phenomenon realistically. The very occurrence of the funeral signifies that death has taken place, life as we know it has drawn to a close. This is an irreversible and irrevocable event. It is a part of man's human condition, for although he can delay death he cannot avoid it ultimately. Man can be truly man only as he faces up to these facts and confronts the reality of death. One of the functions of the funeral is to help him do just this.

Furthermore, the funeral represents a theological understanding of the body of the deceased. Here there must be a concern for proportion. It is possible to have too much or too little regard for the body of the one who has died. From the point of view of the New Testament it is incorrect to see man's existence solely in terms of his physical body. Thus the Christian funeral is not intent upon centering all attention on the corpse, making of it an object of reverence, seeking to maintain the existence of the person by preserving the body ad infinitum. At the same time, the body is regarded as a part of the created order. In the language of Paul, the Christian sees it as the temple of the Holy Spirit. Even in death it represents part of the total person, in no less sense than the nonphysical elements of man. Thus the Christian funeral is not intent upon ignoring the body nor despising it, getting it out of sight or thought as quickly as possible. The Christian funeral seeks to put the body in perspective as a part of the total person who has died.

According to its best understanding the funeral presents resources which the faith offers to meet the needs of the bereaved. It brings a faithful confidence in the present concern and abiding love of God for both living and dead into confrontation with the sense of painful loss, fear, guilt, and confusion in the mourners. The funeral bears witness to the Christian hope for new life beyond death, to the sustaining love of God even amid suffering, and to the strength which God provides for the facing and accepting of reality. This witness is made not only verbally but in the activity of the Christian community, the church, ministering to the bereaved.

The Protestant theological rationale for the funeral contains at least two major themes. First of all the funeral is intended to be a benediction on the deceased, his person and his life. Some churches, particularly in the Anglican and Roman Catholic traditions, interpret this as an occasion for intercessory prayer for the deceased. The prayers for the dead are intended to petition for the salvation of the individual's soul and the improvement of his state beyond death. Most Protestant churches would understand this element of benediction as a passive commitment of the deceased to the mercy of God rather than as active intercession.

One purpose of the funeral defined as benediction involves the respectful and dignified disposition of the body. The mode of disposition is irrelevant at this point. The fact that the funeral has as one of its functions a ceremonial accompaniment for separating the body of the dead from the community of the living is an act of benediction because the body is not summarily discarded. This is in no sense a matter of fearing reprisal from the spirit of the deceased if the body is not buried, as was the case among the ancient Greeks or even the people of the Middle Ages. Rather it is an endeavor to symbolize the ending of a life by enabling the dissolution of the physical matrix in which that life was lived while still indicating an abiding concern and affection for the total person of the deceased. The commitment of the whole person to God is the act of blessing which constitutes one portion of the theological understanding of the purpose of the funeral.

The funeral can be understood as an act of benediction because it stands in the context of the Christian hope for the resurrection. Commending the deceased to God is an act which can be undertaken only in the confidence in the resurrection. The disposition of the body is a symbol of separation from this life, but it is not a consignment to oblivion because of this hope. Actually, it is the confident hope in resurrection which makes it possible to conceive the funeral in terms of benediction.

The second major theme in the theological rationale for the funeral is that of coping with death. The funeral provides a means for dealing with death both in terms of the death of a loved one and of one's own death.

The funeral is, in part, a ritual which seeks to lay a basis for confronting the mystery of death. The emotional trauma that accompanies the death of one with whom we have had a meaningful relationship is quite evident. Coupled with this is a search for some sort of explanation or interpretation which will begin to yield the meaning of death. Death very often brings intense suffering to the bereaved. Suffering becomes more tolerable when we can find some meaning in it. This need for explanation and meaning can be observed in the statements very often made by mourners in the early phases of their bereavement. These statements become so common that one sometimes suspects that they are little more than clichés. "His time had come." "It's God's will." "He's better off now."

The funeral offers a way in which meaningful interpretation of the suffering that comes through loss can be presented. Although the element of mystery cannot be removed from the future, witness can be borne to the faith that the future, like the present, is within the scope of God's power and concern. In spite of the necessary search for answers there can be the confidence that both life and death exist within a structure of meaning.

This coping process is founded upon the hope for the resurrection which is central to the Christian confrontation of death. Although the pain of separation is not allayed, death is a less formidable antagonist when it is seen in the light of the promise of new life. As the funeral bears witness to the Christian hope, the bereaved gain perspective upon the death of their loved one.

The other dimension of the coping process deals with the potency of reflecting upon one's own death. The universality and inevitability of death is never truly shaded by either subtlety or secrecy. Bereavement brings these facts home forcefully. Thus it is that the funeral has the task of assisting the individual to confront this reality.

Herman Feifel has pointed to the way in which the capacity to grasp the concept of a future and of inevitable death is a unique part of human nature. Man does not confront this future with total equanimity. "Death is something that happens to each one of us. Even before its actual arrival, it is an absent presence. Some hold that the fear of death is a universal reaction and that no one is free from it." [16] If this reaction is part of our common humanity, it seems entirely reasonable that such feelings would come closest to the surface when death has caused personal bereavement. Thus the ceremonial context of death and bereavement would have as one of its focuses the possibility for coming to terms with death, even in relationship to one's own death.

The help which the funeral provides for assisting individuals to cope with intimations of their own death naturally varies from person to person. Most commonly, however, it seeks to fulfill this function by providing a structure of meaning which is not totally destroyed by the reality of death and by relating this meaning to life as well as to death. Thus it is not uncommon for funerals to place some emphasis on the need for mourners to examine their own lives and to rededicate themselves to purposes of worth. Even though death involves radical separation from life, the theological understanding of these two realities can never deal with one to the exclusion of the other. The contemplation of death provides something of the quality of our living, and the meaningful regard for our living is preparation for dying. This needs to be seen in more than simple moralistic terms. We cannot assert merely that a person is persuaded to be honest and generous by the thought of his dying. Rather it is a matter of the deepest dimensions of the quality of his living being enriched by the confrontation of the fact of his dying.

The theological dimension of the funeral becomes clearer when we examine the resources which it provides for these tasks. The funeral in both its form and content has been designed to meet needs of the bereaved by making more evident their relationship to God. It is in this relationship that faith,

[16] Herman Feifel, "Death—Relevant Variable in Psychology," *Existential Psychology*, ed. by Rollo May (New York: Random House, 1961), p. 62.

hope, peace, and strength are to be found to meet the crisis situation of death.

In the survey to which earlier reference was made the pastors were offered a series of seven definitions of the funeral arranged at random and asked to rank them from the most adequate to the least adequate. The order in which the majority of the pastors placed the definitions is as follows:

1. The funeral is a worship service which bears witness to the Christian hope in the resurrection.
2. The funeral is a worship service in which God is praised and thanked for the blessings of life.
3. The funeral is a worship service in which God's gracious help is sought in a time of crisis.
4. The funeral is a gathering of a concerned community of friends, neighbors, and family to manifest shared sorrow.
5. The funeral is a means of commemorating the life of one who has been known and loved.
6. The funeral is a service to lend a fitting conclusion to life.
7. The funeral is a ceremonial means for disposing of a dead body with dignity and propriety.

The high level of unanimity is shown in the fact that definition number 1 was ranked first by 70 percent of the ministers and second or third by an additional 20 percent. Definition number 2 was ranked first through fourth by 98 percent. Definition number 7 was ranked in last place by 59 percent and next to last by an additional 11 percent. When these rankings were tabulated on a denominational rather than a regional basis no truly significant differences were noted.

The fact that the most acceptable definitions describe the funeral as a service of worship lays emphasis upon the relational aspect of the Christian definition of the funeral. It is an activity which is undertaken consciously in the context of relationship with God. The outgrowths of this relationship are then seen in terms of the remainder of the definition: bearing

111

witness to the hope in the resurrection, praising and thanking God for the blessings of life, and seeking God's help in time of crisis.

The faith which is fostered through the funeral is not just a matter of some kind of intellectual understanding about life and death. It is not merely an acceptance of some dogmatic statements about life after death. Faith is rather an attitude in which one trusts in the goodness of God even in the face of suffering. It is confidence in God's ordering of life and death. It is assurance of God's unending providence. It is an acceptance of strength beyond the measure of one's own resources, knowing that one faces the crisis in relationship with the Creator and Sustainer of all being.

The presentation of hope is one of the purposes of the funeral when it is understood in its theological dimension. In the language of the New Testament this is the hope for the resurrection of the dead. It is the confident expectation that God gives new life beyond the ending of this existence. This hope again grows out of relationship to the Source of being.

In addition to this the funeral, seen in its theological dimension, is a means by which one who is lacerated by loss can find a measure of peace. This peace must not be thought of as an escape from the reality of suffering. It is not an analgesic which covers the pain. Perhaps it is better to think of this peace in terms of poise. It is a stance in which one who suffers finds the poise to confront and accept the impact of suffering and to endure it to the point of overcoming. In the light of what we have already said of man's inherent fear of death, such peace can come only through a resource that is not produced by the individual himself.

The funeral is also intended to impart strength. This is the original meaning of comfort: to make strong. Contrary to our popular usage of the word, we cannot comfort a man by taking his burden from him but by strengthening him to endure it. Much has already been written of the well-intentioned harm done to mourners by seeking to divert them from their crisis rather than by helping them to endure and overcome it. The resources of which we have been speaking are all intended to provide new strength for the bereaved person.

Again we would point out that the context in which this strength is given is the context of relationship—relationship with God and also relationship with fellow mourners. One of the intentions of the funeral, seen in its theological dimension, is that it is a service of worship in which those who mourn the death of a loved one are joined by a congregation of concerned persons who share, insofar as they are able, the loss and pain.

A Multidimensional Pattern for Defining the Funeral

On the basis of this examination of the understanding of the funeral in these four dimensions we are now in a position to join together the contributions which each makes to a definition of the funeral. As indicated at the beginning of this chapter this definition will be multidimensional.

Cultural anthropology understands the funeral as a means of coping with death and the effect of death upon the deceased, the mourners, and the social group. It provides a rationale for regarding the deceased as one of the important focuses of the funeral.

Social psychology understands the funeral as a ritual in which the social group provides support for the individual mourner by expressing its solidarity. The funeral also expresses the way in which the group finds meaning in the changes which the death of one of its members brings about, both in terms of the ending of relationship and its continuation on a new basis.

Psychology understands the funeral as a public ritual which is a part of the process of the emotional reorientation of the mourner to life without the former quality of relationship

113

with the deceased. It regards the funeral as one of the ways for meeting the psychological needs of the bereaved, giving sanction to their need to accept reality and to express and assimilate their feelings toward that reality.

Theology understands the funeral as a service of worship which witnesses to the context of relationship with God in which both life and death are regarded. Thus it provides a specific content for many of the symbolic meanings which were referred to in the other dimensions. In seeking to understand death within the context of relationship with God it finds in the funeral an occasion for testifying to the hope in the resurrection from the dead, for praising and thanking God for his providence in life and death, and for seeking God's help in time of crisis.

The interrelationship among these various dimensions of definition of the funeral is not simple. It is quite obvious that there is considerable overlapping of elements within. Perhaps it would be more adequate to say that these various dimensions interpenetrate. Although some of them may appear to elaborate others, it should not be assumed that one is basic and others derivative. Yet each dimension adds something to the total picture which the others do not provide.

As a basis for our continuing discussion of the funeral in subsequent chapters this diagram (Figure 1) is proposed as one helpful way to understanding the relationship of these dimensions in seeking to define the funeral.

Evaluating the Funeral

This entire study is based on the assumption that it is possible to evaluate objectively the effectiveness of the funeral in a number of ways. Whenever evaluation is undertaken, the danger is present that judgment will be consciously or unconsciously affected by the pressure of vested interest. It is quite possible that funeral interests would find it difficult to be objective because of their economic involvement in funeral practices. It is possible that the church would lose objectivity because of a desire to defend one of the traditional functions of the religious community. It is possible that the judgment of an individual who sought to escape from the painful realities of death and bereavement might be lacking in objectivity. And so the question of the effectiveness of the

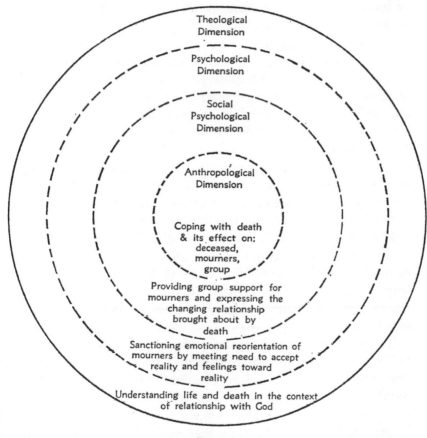

Figure 1
A Model for Defining the Funeral
in Several Dimensions

115

funeral cannot be adequately decided without the establishment of suitable norms.

Just as individual behavior is full of meaning due to the conscious or unconscious dimensions of the past experience of the person, so cultural phenomena reflect the collective experience of the group. Funerals, for example, reflect a people's reaction to death, their hierarchy of values and threats of loss, their world view, their religious understanding of life and death or the absence of such a view, their status in life. The slave looked forward to crossing over Jordan into the land of promise, while the sensate culture of the twentieth century anxiously anticipates dreadful oblivion.

It cannot be denied that present-day funerals may appear to have been cut off from their original purposes. Many of them are perfunctory. Custom has enabled them to be used as superficial insulators. There is widespread lack of authentic participation. More and more it is possible to see funerals reflecting some of the neurotic solutions of the culture—illusion, extreme materialism, and insulation from deep feeling. Certainly there is much within the modern funeral which stimulates dissatisfaction for the thoughtful person.

It could be argued that since our culture has produced the contemporary funeral it should be regarded as a valid expression of modern man's sense of his own need. We cannot, however, forget that the funeral may also reflect the limitations, even the sickness, of a culture. Again the need for norms is readily apparent.

To apply one criterion to a subject makes judgment relatively simple. Either the subject measures up to the norm or it does not. To apply a variety of criteria, representative of a number of different perspectives, will not make evaluating more simple, but it should increase the effectiveness of the judgment. It is for this reason that norms based upon somewhat diverse disciplines have been proposed by this study and are summarized here.

Social Norms for the Funeral

Some of the norms grow out of the social-psychological investigation of the effect of bereavement on the individual within the context of a group.

1. *An adequate funeral should provide an opportunity for the manifestation of shared loss and a means by which the support of the community of mourners is conveyed to the bereaved.* The funeral in the truest sense of the word is a social function, representing the solidarity of the group relationship in time of crisis.

2. *The funeral should express social understanding of the relationship of the living to those who have died.* Although this naturally refers most immediately to the person whose death has occasioned the funeral, it also refers to relationship to those who have died in time past. The funeral can offer a way in which the group, while thoroughly acknowledging a state of "having died," still maintains certain kinds of ritual connections with the dead.

3. *The funeral should begin the process of strengthening relational patterns among the living.* The funeral is a part of the extended process of reorienting the relationships of life to adjust to the loss of relationship brought about by death. This does not mean that actual relationships growing out of the funeral need to be the direct means of healing. Rather it means that the strength which is drawn from accepting relationships in the funeral indicates to the bereaved that it is in relationship that a new orientation to life will be found.

Psychological Norms for the Funeral

Another group of norms emerges from the study of psychology as it understands the effect of bereavement upon the individual.

1. *The funeral should assist in the reinforcement of reality*

117

for the bereaved. Without such reinforcement the whole painful process of mourning seems purposeless and without meaning.

2. *The funeral should aid the necessary recollection of the deceased and the beginning of the recapitulation of the relationship.* Although the funeral does dramatically mark separation, it also marks the need for relationship in the dimension of memory. This is not a desperate effort to hold on to the deceased but is a way of maintaining a different order of relationship.

3. *The funeral by conveying the element of finality in death should eventuate in the freedom for developing new relational patterns without violation of the integrity of previous relationship with the deceased.* The funeral is one of the most effective means for portraying the paradox of the ending of relationship as it has been known and the establishment of a different dimension of relationship based upon recollection. Without this paradox the mourner is caught in a dilemma: either he must cut himself off totally from the deceased, virtually wiping out a significant part of his past life, or he must stay bound in an illusory relationship which fails to recognize that a radical separation has taken place.

4. *The funeral should offer an opportunity for the release of authentic feelings.* The possibility of such release in the context of relationship is doubly helpful because it not only provides catharsis but also offers the occasion for acceptance of the person as he really feels.

Theological Norms for the Funeral

Yet another group of norms can be formulated on the basis of the theological understandings of death and bereavement seen in the context of man's relationship to God.

1. *The funeral should enable mourners to be more meaningfully related to religious resources for the understanding and*

118

acceptance of suffering. A glib and superficial assertion, "It is the will of God," will accomplish little. A more helpful understanding will seek meaning in the confidence that God's providence encompasses all existence and that the Christian community participates in this providing for the needs of the mourners.

2. *The funeral should, at least in rudimentary form, develop a perspective on the meaning of life and death in the light of the present crisis.* Although the emotional shock of loss has to subside somewhat before such perspective is attainable, the mourner confronts the coming together of life and death in his own experience. He is virtually compelled to face the possibility of his own death and is thus driven to probe the meaning of his life. The funeral should place this task in a context of relationship with God.

3. *The funeral should assist the mourners intellectually and emotionally to comprehend more fully the nature of man as a unity of body and spirit.* This is not merely a matter of developing and supporting abstract ideas. This issue is absolutely crucial for mourners in answering both explicit and implicit questions regarding the disposition of the body, the possibility and impossibility of continued relationship with the deceased, and the existence of the deceased after death.

The Potentiality of the Funeral

It certainly must be acknowledged that the modern funeral does not meet all of these norms adequately. Some propose that the funeral, therefore, be regarded as a failure and be discontinued or replaced. Others would suggest that greater effort be made to apply suitable norms constructively to the funeral in such a way as to make it more helpful to bereaved individuals and societies.

Even those who have been highly critical of the funeral have posited a day when many of these values were met in the funeral.[17] Once the funeral fulfilled useful purposes, but not now. The reason advanced for this often has been that funeral practices have been perverted by those economically interested in the funeral. This point cannot be wholly denied, but there are a number of other important reasons for the failure of contemporary funerals to approach the norms more fully. We have already pointed to a number of these.

Modern man has changed his view of death, has sought to hide from its reality, has divorced it from life, has denied its significance for life. The social processes of urbanization and industrialization have created an impersonal way of life in which meaningful relationships are reduced to the point that loss is minimized. The de-sacralization of life has limited the dimensions in which man regards his own being to super-ficialities rather than enabling him to grasp the real depth of his being. The sophistication of our time has blinded man to the possibility of real meaning being conveyed through ritual. All of these factors contribute to the decreased effectiveness of the funeral.

The fundamental questions which we must ask are these: Have the needs of the bereaved individual and the disrupted society changed? In contrast to any time in the past is there any less need now to face reality? Is there any less need to accept the finality of death? Is there any less need for the support of a group which shares loss? Is there less need to have regard for the whole man? Is there less need to remember the deceased and to be emancipated from past relationship through memory? Is there less need to gain a meaningful perspective on both life and death?

There seems to be far less reason for assuming that these basic needs have been altered than for supposing that resources which can meet these needs have been neglected or super-seded. There is no need to look with longing for a return of

[17] Jessica Mitford, *The American Way of Death*, p. 199; Ruth M. Harmer, *The High Cost of Dying*, pp. 44, 225 f.

yesterday. A serious effort does need to be made to assess the resources within the individual himself, within the social group, within the community of faith. Many of these resources can be activated by the funeral, properly understood and conducted.

Both anthropology and theology, although in somewhat different ways, acknowledge that ritual has a dual relationship to the values which find expression through it. On the one hand the symbols which are involved in ritual convey and bear witness to the values and meanings of the group. At the same time the symbols present in ritual exercise an influence on these values. Ritual, then, is not merely a reflection of meaning but can also be a way of shaping meanings. It is thus reasonable to hope that the possibility for restoring proper goals for the funeral may bring about the reform and renewal of important values and meanings associated with life and death in contemporary culture.

Facing death realistically is the major objective from which all others follow. From several fronts this objective is being sought. In contemporary literature, art, and philosophy the existentialist solution is offered. It is proposed that only the confrontation of death brings a new confrontation of the present life. Only as man acknowledges death as a part of life and faces his very own death does true authenticity come into his living. He learns in this way truly to care for others. He begins to appreciate the depth which is possible in the relationships of life. His life becomes filled with purposeful contributions to ongoing existence.

The Christian solution also calls for an honest facing of death. It includes that which has just been described, with two important differences. It bases authentic existence not on the raw courage that comes through facing death but upon the relationship with God which enables a confrontation with both life and death. It does not limit authenticity to present existence, although it is involved there, but also states it in terms of a new life which overcomes death. The context is one of continuing contact with reality rather than annihilation or oblivion even for the brave.

The funeral remains as the major avenue for the reconstruction of modern man's view of death. At the present time, in spite of its inadequacies, it is still a part of the common experience of most persons. It possesses a capacity for acute involvement which other effective forms of communication, such as literature or art, may not have. The funeral has the potentialities for meeting the needs of bereaved individuals and communities.

6

Lines of Demarcation

If the funeral is defined multidimensionally, then it is quite possible that a way can be found for conducting funerals in different dimensions.

The diagram (Figure 1) which was presented in the last chapter (p. 115) sought to describe the various dimensions of the function and meaning of the funeral as a series of concentric circles. Each one of these dimensions, because it is closely related to an element of the function of the funeral, can be regarded as a thing in itself or can be seen as a portion of a composite picture of the funeral. There is no standard or "correct" pattern for the blending of these various dimensions. For purposes of discussion and explanation, they have been diagramed as accumulating from the inside circle outward.

In Figure 2 several segments (A, B, C, D) have been drawn on the diagram to indicate ways in which dimensions can be combined to increase the scope of the function and meaning of the funeral. Again it should be pointed out that the regular progression described by these expanding segments does not indicate a necessary or inevitable combination. The major purpose of this diagram is to show that the more dimensions a funeral includes, the more potentially effective it will be.

Let us see what these expanding segments would provide in the funeral. The segment marked A represents a funeral which is understood only as a coping function. In its least complicated form it would be only a matter of disposing of the body of the deceased. Man can hardly bring himself just to discard a corpse unless he is trying to bring ignominy on the person. Some simple or more elaborate form of disposition

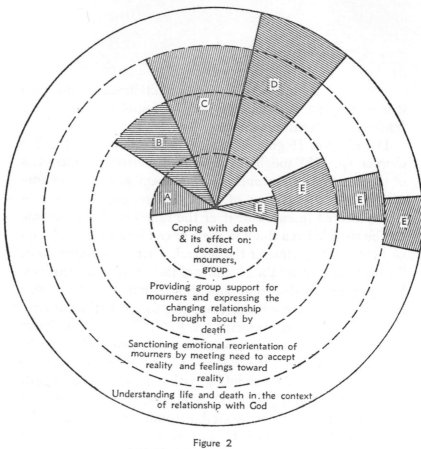

Figure 2
A Model of the Scope of the Function
and Meaning of the Funeral

is a part of the coping function. Coping very often also involves some effort to deal with death by seeking a means to revitalize the dead. The form by which this is sought may vary a great deal. It may be the prehistoric magical efforts to denote new life by covering the bones with red ochre powder. It may be the primitive attempt to equip the corpse with all the necessary equipment for living—the grave goods of food, tools, weapons. It may be the more contemporary endeavor to give a corpse the appearance of life in a neurotic attempt to cope with the reality of death by denying it. It may be the death-defying Christian affirmation of resurrection. In a sense, the whole endeavor to cope with death in the funeral is in some way tied to the question of whether one will face and accept the reality of death or avoid and deny it. It would be possible, although it is not likely, that a funeral could be conducted entirely as a coping function.

The segment designated *B* indicates a funeral that deals with two dimensions. It seeks to fulfill its function not only by coping with the reality of death but also by offering group participation. The individual mourner does not have to meet death alone but in company with others who share his loss in part and who support him during the period of disorganization due to the impact of death. The group, through its rituals, helps to interpret to him something of the meaning of what is taking place. It tries to help him see that while the one who has died will be missed, life can and must go on. It seeks to convey the possibility for maintaining a relationship to the departed member of the group through memory and commemoration. It strives to respect the separation from the group life which the mourner feels and to smooth the way for his return to normal group participation. The funeral then is a corporate act in which the group seeks to offer its resources to the members with the greatest need in that crisis.

The segment marked *C* depicts a funeral which includes three dimensions. All that is stated above pertains, but there is included an emphasis upon the function of the funeral in meeting the needs of the mourner to deal with his feelings toward the reality in which he finds himself. The group shows its understanding of what the mourner is experiencing and its willingness to accept him along with all his feelings. The funeral is an occasion in which the group lends its sanction to the expression of his feelings. In a sense, the group helps the individual to free his own psychic resources for dealing with the strong emotions which occur in bereavement.

Section D indicates the funeral which has its function in four dimensions. The innovation here is the theological dimension which places all of the previously described functions into the context of the relationship of man with God. The Christian understanding of life and death and the affirmation of the hope for the resurrection become the basis of the coping function. The church, the Christian community, becomes the supportive group which shares the mourner's sorrow and provides him with the ritual in which he is able to find the meanings through which life and death and all that they entail are understood. The relationship to God and to other members of the Christian community provides the acceptance which frees the mourner to confront the reality of his crisis and to express honestly his feeling toward it. The reorientation of life without the presence of the deceased is accomplished in the context of relationship with God.

Before leaving the diagram we should note that it would be entirely possible, although not likely, that the funeral could be limited to one dimension only. This is indicated with any one of the segments marked E. A funeral might be only a group gathering together to commemorate the death of a member with no theological reference at all. Or a funeral might be only a religious ritual with no awareness of or relevance to the psychological needs of the mourners.

The position which is being advanced here is this: *the adequacy of a funeral is increased in direct proportion to the number of dimensions which are involved.* Our point of view is that the most adequate funeral involves all of the dimensions. However, funerals which deal with only some of the dimensions are nevertheless helpful, although to a lesser degree.

Three Types of Funerals

One of the problems that is deeply involved in the American funeral is that the funeral is seen as "religious" even by those who are not religious themselves. Even though a survey conducted by Robert L. Fulton[1] indicated that scarcely more than 10 percent of those polled saw the primary function of the contemporary funeral as religious, there are minimal "religious" conditions that normally need to be met. These are usually of a very superficial nature. The form should be the form of a religious service although the content is a matter of indifference. The sine qua non seems to be the participation of some clergyman. Very few funerals are held without the presence of a minister. Whether this represents vestiges of Western tradition which has regarded the funeral exclusively as a religious service or represents the absence in our society of anyone other than a clergyman to conduct burial rituals is difficult to say.

Thus it is that pastors are called upon not only to conduct funeral services for their parishioners but also to officiate at the burial of people who are not members of the church or who have no apparent commitment to the faith. If the mourners sincerely desire a Christian ministry to bring a measure of comfort to them, this is one thing. But all too often that pastor under such circumstances has little or no contact with the bereaved family apart from the funeral hour. They have had no previous acquaintance with him, and they may never see him again. His ministry to them is extremely limited by these conditions. The pastor sometimes feels, with consider-

[1] Robert L. Fulton, The Sacred and the Secular: Attitudes of the American Public Toward Death (Milwaukee: Bulfin Printers, 1963), p. 2.

able justification, that he is operating as a mere functionary rather than as a minister.

It is not unusual in such instances, particularly in larger communities, for a family to request the funeral director to secure the services of a minister for them. He makes all the necessary arrangements with the pastor, again reducing the opportunity for contact with the bereaved. Some pastors have responded agreeably to such circumstances either because they feel that they should use every possible means for being of service to those who wish the ministry of the church or because their congregations have set salary scales at a level that requires income from such adjunct ministries. Other pastors are extremely uncomfortable in those circumstances where they can detect no apparent reason for participation as a minister other than being a kind of community shaman to satisfy convention. To them this ministry seems empty and somewhat meaningless.

An overview of the American funeral leads us to suggest that the assumption that the funeral is a religious service is not wholly correct. It would seem more accurate to categorize three types of funerals.

First of all, there is the *religious funeral*. This funeral is essentially oriented in a religious community. Although we are examining the funeral primarily from the position of Protestant Christianity, in our pluralistic society we would recognize in this category also funerals that are conducted in non-Christian traditions. These would include American elements of the great world religions, such as Judaism, Buddhism, and others, which sustain a community and function through the rituals of that community. The other major portion of this first category would include the funerals which are conducted in the Christian tradition, Protestant, Roman Catholic, Anglican, and Orthodox. It is assumed that the deceased was a part of the religious community in which this service takes place and that the mourners have a basic regard for that community of faith. It is assumed that there is a genuine desire to mark the conclusion of a life within the context of the faith and hope and fellowship of this religious community.

The second type of funeral could be called the *conventional funeral*. On the surface, it may seem very little different from the service described above. However, it is arranged and conducted largely because in our society it is customary to have some "religious" rites when death occurs. There is no viable relationship between the deceased or his family and a community of faith. So in order to meet the social expectations a representative of the church and some of its ritual elements need to be imported. For the people involved, this is a pseudo-religious ceremony which is symptomatic of religion-in-general in its most superficial form. It employs ritual acts which are devoid of meaning for the mourners because they are foreign to the community which invests that ritual with meaning. It may be motivated only by a desire to maintain appearances, to do the things one ought to do. Or it may be motivated by a deeper desire to find the help which traditionally comes through the ritual of a people to bring a sense of meaning into a crisis situation. But the ritual fails the mourners because they are alien to the structure of meaning and to the community which propounds it.

A third type of funeral is fairly uncommon. We might speak of it as the *humanistic funeral*. It is a ritual which is frankly nontheistic in both structure and content. Rather than reflecting the ritual and meaning of a community of faith in the religious sense, it seeks to reflect the faith of the secular community in man's nature and capability. Its position is expressed: "The Humanist view rejects the idea of personal immortality and interprets death as the final end of the individual conscious personality. The philosophy of religion of Humanism sets up the happiness and progress of mankind on this earth as the supreme goal of human endeavor." [2] A ritual is developed which seeks to carry the meaning of this philosophy and assumes that those who carry out the ritual are committed to this system of meaning.

The humanistic funeral is at present found only infrequently in our experience. It is carried out usually in the context of a small group which is self-consciously humanistic and frankly nonreligious. On the American scene the vast majority of funerals would fall into the first two categories—the religious and the conventional.

The Problem of the Conventional Funeral

American Protestantism acknowledges this phenomenon as something of a problem. The survey which was taken of more than a hundred pastors from various areas of the nation and from a variety of major denominations indicated some of the ways in which efforts are made to deal with this distinction between religious (in this case, Christian) and conventional funerals.

A rather small group of the pastors polled indicated that this was no particular problem for them because they consistently refused to conduct funerals for other than their own parishioners or those who had made profession of the Christian faith. In a few instances this was church policy, although more often it was a matter of the personal policy of the pastor. He did not necessarily imply an adverse judgment on those outside the Christian faith but so conceived his role that there was no rationale for his participation in the conventional funeral.

Another position did not limit itself quite so much but set officially sanctioned terms for participating in funerals for those who were not a part of the community of faith. Some

[2] Corliss Lamont, A Humanist Funeral Service (New York: Horizon Press, 1954), p. 8.

churches have specific policies that funerals shall not be held in the church building for those who were not professing Christians. In some instances there are special funeral rituals for "The Burial of Those Who Die Without the Sign of Faith."

A much more widely held position involves the pastor's unofficial, personally established conditions for conducting conventional funerals. Most often this is done by modifying the funeral service which is normally used for professing Christians. The scripture lessons and prayers are selected in such a way that the focus is much more general than specific. The emphasis on the hope for the resurrection is not given the same stress as it is in the traditional church service. The whole approach to the funeral is less personal, partly because of lack of acquaintance with the deceased and the mourners and partly because the focus of the funeral is almost fully on the mourners and their needs. A sizable number of pastors indicated that their funerals for nonparishioners were impersonal and general, not because of disdain for the deceased or the mourners, but because the specific emphases of the Christian ritual were somewhat irrelevant to those who do not share in the meanings of the community of faith.

Still another position places no limitations and enables the minister to conduct funerals for all who request his services. About a third of the pastors polled indicated that they made no significant difference in the services which they conducted for parishioners and for those outside the church. There appear to be three major rationales for this position.

First, some of these pastors see the funeral in terms of a total emphasis on the living. Their approach is not affected by the religious status of the deceased. An effort is made to bring a measure of comfort to those who mourn by assuring them of God's concern for them. Some of these pastors welcome this as an opportunity for evangelization of the mourners, feeling that to serve nonmembers may establish a fruitful point of contact between them and the church.

A second rationale is that the pastor is not in a position to assume responsibility for judging the religious status of the deceased or the mourners. Church membership or humanitarian acts are regarded as deceptive criteria for such a judgment. Since judgment cannot be rendered by a man, the pastor deals humbly with all who seek his ministry. He regards the funeral service as sufficiently objective to be used in all instances without compromising its substance. The pastor prefers to err on the side of overextension of the ministry of the church rather than on the side of accepting the responsibility for arbitrarily judging who is qualified to receive this ministry.

The third rationale is, hopefully, uncommon. It is based upon the assumption that the funeral really isn't too important anyway. At its worst, this is a lack of integrity which says that the symbols in the Christian ritual are devoid of meaning. At its best, it sees the meanings in such generalized terms that they are equally relevant to parishioners or to those who have no part in the community of faith which has presented those meanings.

The picture of the American funeral has to include recognition of the categories of religious, conventional, and humanistic. At the same time it must be admitted that there is clearcut definition only on the ends of this continuum. The broad middle category is not differentiated with any clarity and tends to blend itself into the religious understanding of the funeral.

This lack of clear definition and differentiation poses many problems for the church, for the culture, and for the funeral itself. It has been true for centuries that pseudoreligion is always more destructive to the church than is pure secularism. Since its inception, the church has resisted any form of religiosity motivated only by a desire for social acceptability. It has laid emphasis upon personal involvement and commitment, whether this is couched in terms of "following the Master" or "ultimate concern."

The church has not been unwilling to serve the needs of men outside its community of faith, but it has not served merely to give the flavoring of religiosity to life outside the church. Thus the conventional funeral, patricularly when it is undefined, is a danger to the integrity of the church. It constitutes a form of cultural accommodation. It fits into the popular espousal of religion-in-general which assumes that the presence of a functionary connected with a religious body and the use of the language or forms of a religious group are sufficient to make something religious. In its most extreme form this might be seen in the "hiring" of a minister as a part of the unofficial staff of a funeral establishment to "take care of" funerals for people without church affiliation.

Through this kind of accommodation it is possible that the Christian meaning of the funeral may be lost. This is an extremely delicate issue because it is so easy to appear to be self-righteous or judgmental or legalistic when dealing with it. We should be clear that there is no sense in which a Christian or even a religious funeral has a salutary effect upon the deceased. There are no efficacious formulas that need to be given to believers nor withheld from unbelievers. The funeral is not understood as imparting grace in the sacramental sense by any part of the Christian church. Thus any effort to construe the funeral as a weapon for church discipline or a lever for pressuring people toward commitment is totally out of place. The issue is not one of granting a Christian funeral to bestow a favor upon the individual or withholding a Christian funeral to indicate reprobation. The issue simply is: Can the Christian funeral fulfill a useful function for those who lack in commitment or understanding a basis for meaningful participation? It is apparent that without such a basis the funeral would seem to be irrelevant except as a mere means for satisfying convention.

There is a purely practical problem posed here. How will the church and the pastor decide whether a Christian or a humanistic funeral is indicated? We must recognize that this is not always an easy decision, because in many cases persons are nominal Christians or may have been estranged from the church for various reasons. The temptation would often be to draw a line according to external standards, such as membership in good standing, record of contribution or attendance, and personal conduct. The standard we propose here is much more complex. The decision is to be reached in each instance on the basis of an assessment of the major mourners' capacity for finding relevant meaning in the Christian funeral. Some of the questions which need to be faced are: Is the orientation of the major mourners theistic or humanistic? Is there some indication that there will be in the major mourners a personal response to the meaning of the hope for resurrection as a gift of new life from God or would it, at best, have meaning only as some kind of universal immortality that is a part of man's nature? Would the fellowship of the Christian congregation have any more meaning for them than the assembling of sympathetic friends? Would the funeral be meaningful as a service of worship or would it be only a community gathering to pay tribute to the deceased?

If the church accepts the premise that its mission is to serve all men, then these assessments can be made with humility because through them the church will seek the way in which these particular mourners can best be served according to their own structure of meanings.

The pseudoreligious nature of the conventional funeral also creates problems within the culture. The church, as a part of the culture in which it exists, has certain resources and values which it contributes to the culture. The Christian funeral is one of the means by which many individuals in the culture are helped to confront bereavement. If such a resource is superficially regarded or diluted, its worth to the culture is significantly reduced. Simply put, religion-in-general has a lesser contribution to make to the culture than a faith which is solidly oriented in the belief and commitment of the Christian church. The pseudoreligious funeral will not advance the helpful possibilities of the religious funeral but will subvert it by making it seem a hollow shell, judged to be without value.

It should not be assumed that religion-in-general represents an ideal compromise in the situation of pluralism which is now finally being recognized in our culture. The problems posed by pluralism will be met by ecumenism, dialogue, and coexistence rather than by reduction to a general common denominator.

Our American culture has traditionally looked to the church for assistance in meeting the crisis of death. It has been served as the church has offered its ritual to convey the Christian meaning of life and death. But if these meanings are cut off from their roots, if they are empty symbols, neither church nor culture nor individual is served.

The funeral itself is also harmed by the pseudoreligious quality of the conventional funeral. This is a result of the presupposition that all funerals must be religious. In an effort to accommodate this assumption the vast majority of funerals have adopted some of the forms of a religious service with little regard for whether or not there is a basis for reception of the meaning of those symbols on the part of the bereaved. Because of this disjuncture between the symbols of the Christian funeral and the capacity for reception in persons who have no viable commitment to the faith, it is small wonder that the funeral has been found by many to be sterile structure and irrelevant ritual. This certainly is a part of the reason for suggestions that the funeral be abandoned as a barren anachronism.

It has too often been assumed that because the religious funeral lacks meaning for some in terms of its symbols, it is therefore completely worthless and expendable. Here we need to recall what was said earlier about the various dimensions of definition which could be applied to the funeral (cf. p. 113).

There is always the possibility for a confused or partial understanding of the funeral and its function. If our earlier assumption is true, that the adequacy of the funeral is increased in direct proportion to the number of dimensions which are involved, we recognize that satisfactory fulfillment of the function in one dimension does not necessarily mean a funeral that is wholly adequate to the needs of the participants. But at the same time it indicates that lack of meaning in one area does not necessarily infer lack of meaning in all areas of the funeral.

Given the situation in our culture, it is expecting too much to assume that all funerals will involve all of the dimensions and therefore be totally adequate. However, even reduced adequacy does not mean total uselessness. Partial fulfillment of the function of the funeral is vastly superior to the complete absence of this function.

A Proposed Solution

On the basis of this kind of understanding, we would advance the serious proposal that there be *frank acceptance of two types of funerals: religious and humanistic*. What we have referred to as the conventional funeral would find no place in such an understanding. It would be seen as an anomalous compromise between the two legitimate types of funerals.

The religious funeral would have as its basis the theological dimension of the function of the funeral as providing an understanding of life and death in the context of relationship with God. It would add the other dimensions of the meaning of the funeral, increasing its adequacy with each addition. The symbols which have meaning within the context of the faith would make it possible to cope with death and its effects. The community of faith would provide the supportive group.

The climate within this group would sanction and enable the dealing with reality and the feelings which that reality evokes.

The humanistic funeral would involve any combination of the dimensions of the funeral except the theological. It would offer a humanistic, philosophical basis for coping with death. It would provide a sympathetic group to lend support in a situation of common loss. It would assist in the emotional reorientation of the bereaved. Its adequacy would be enhanced with each additional dimension.

By religious we mean to describe attitudes and actions which recognize that life is wholly lived in a context of relationship with God. A more precise term would be theistic, but in order to make this proposal as understandable as possible we shall use the more popular term "religious." My original intention was to counterpoise the term "secular." But this, as we shall see shortly, is not really possible. Rather, the word "humanistic" commends itself. It does not refer to that which has no relation to the church but describes attitudes and actions which acknowledge no dimension of life other than man and the resources that are part of his own nature.

The Tension Between Sacred and Secular

At one time the distinction between sacred and secular was very definite. When the period of the Enlightenment brought a dissolution of the medieval synthesis, there resulted a clear differentiation of spheres of influence of church, state, university, and economic structure. The religious was elevated and relegated to a position of lofty irrelevancy, having little to do with the maneuverings of political, commercial, and scientific powers in the arena where men live.

Many theologians of our day reject this clear distinction between the religious and secular. Representative of this position is Bonhoeffer, who wrote:

137

The division of the total reality in a sacred and a profane sphere, a Christian and a secular sphere, creates the possibility of existence in a single one of these spheres; a spiritual existence which has no part in secular existence, and a secular part which can claim autonomy for itself and can exercise this right of autonomy in its dealings with the spiritual sphere. . . . There are not two spheres, but only one sphere of realization of Christ, in which the reality of God and of the world, which has been accomplished in Christ, is repeated, or more exactly, is realized, ever afresh in the life of men. And yet what is Christian is not identical with what is of the world.[3]

This tendency of modern Christian thought to invalidate the radical distinction between the sacred and the secular fulfills a number of purposes. It does seek to prevent the kind of compartmentalization of life which obviates Christian concern for all segments of existence. It affirms that all of life is related to God, even though there may not be universal awareness of this relationship. It avoids a disavowal of the natural and the insulating of the Christian man from this part of reality through the refinements of asceticism and puritanism. The Christian should not think in terms of areas of existence which are unrelated to God.

In this sense the secular is "the world" or "worldly," but not in the sense of being cut off from God by God, operating outside the sphere of God's power and love. God is present in the world, active in the secular, just as in that which is regarded as the religious. There cannot be any sense of judgmental superiority on the part of the religious, because God is no less present in any part of his creation.

This recalls the distinction made by Troeltsch between two understandings of the church—the church-type and the sect-type. The church-type was conscious of the church as an identifiable body but saw it enfolding and permeating the

[3] Dietrich Bonhoeffer, *Ethics*, ed. Eberhard Bethge, trans. by Neville Smith (New York: The Macmillan Company, 1955), pp. 63 ff.

whole world. There was Christian concern for all sectors of life. In a sense, the church was not only in the world, but the world was also in the church. The sect-type was also very conscious of the church as an identifiable body but maintained this identity through carefully defined boundaries. The church was removed, distant, isolated from the world. Its motion was centripetal, drawing in toward its center and withdrawing as much as possible from the world.

It is important to note, however, that in each of these types there is a clear sense of identity in the church. The same can be said for those in our time who, like Bonhoeffer, point to the need to avoid compartmentalization into sacred and secular realms.

Our proposals for a religious and a humanistic funeral should not be seen as an attempt to reestablish divisions. The involvement of God in all reality, in all sectors of life and death, is presupposed. But at the same time, it must be admitted that some men acknowledge the presence of God while others do not. Some consciously participate in relationship with God while others do not.

Consequently, there is a *de facto* secularization; that is, men may live under the assumption that they are self-sufficient and have no relationship with God. The Christian's traditional view of death has been affected by the religious meanings he has seen in it. Death is understood as the natural terminus of life, but also it is accepted as a part of the divinely ordered universe. With the nontheistic stance of the social sciences and medicine, death has come to be interpreted in a different way for many individuals. It is seen as a problem similar to an illness that is being conquered by medical research. Or it may be understood as an event with no larger significance, roughly equivalent to the dying of an animal or a tree.

Marking the occurrence of death obviously has a different meaning in these two points of view. The symbols of an individual and the society within which he functions reflect the world view and the man view which they hold. Religious ritual symbolically reflects man's sense of relationship with God, whose care and concern extends to both the living and the dead. Humanistic ritual expresses the values which are found in the life of man and the community in which he lives. Religious meanings are absent from and irrelevant to the second position.

Thus when we apply the categories of religious and humanistic to the funeral two dimensions emerge, each with its own set of meanings. Christian meanings describe what the Christian regards as the totality of being, for no part of existence is considered to be apart from God. Both church and world represent spheres in which God is concerned and active. Meanings must therefore be comprehensive, including all of life, death, and the possibility of new life.

Humanistic meanings are also concerned with what the secularist regards as the totality of being, but he draws the boundaries more closely. There is no effort to include a transcendent dimension either in terms of an extension beyond man's being or of profound depth within man's being. The measure of these meanings is man's estimate of himself, the value of his present life and his capacity to find fulfillment in relationship to others. There is little question that these meanings are valid and valuable in the light of their definition of reality.

Now if both these dimensions and their meanings are acknowledged, this means that it is possible to have either a religious (in the context of this study, Christian) funeral or a humanistic funeral. Each fulfills its purpose in its own way. These purposes, as we shall see later, are not identical nor must they be seen as equally comprehensive.

This proposal for a humanistic funeral should not be regarded as an abdication by the church from the funeral nor is it to be seen as a means of setting up competition for the church (or at least for the minister) by turning over some of its present function to a totally secular agent. The Christian funeral, we affirm, belongs in the context of the faith and practice of the community of the Christian church. (The same thing could be said of any other religious body.) We are not advocating "the secularization of one more sector of life." This is nothing more than the acknowledgment of and reaction to a secularism which is already in existence. It is just a stripping away of the disguise of the conventional funeral and the frank recognition that the relevancy of the funeral depends on the climate of receptivity which exists in the mourners for the determination of whether religious or humanistic symbols shall be used. Actually, this proposal for a humanistic funeral is no more vitiating the church than is voluntary attendance of Sunday worship.

In some ways this is quite similar to the situation that already pertains regarding marriage. Persons with a religious orientation are married according to the tradition and meanings of their community of faith. Those whose orientation is humanistic can be married by a civil officer. Both ceremonies are acknowledged by the state as legal. For the most part, the church acknowledges as legitimate the civil ceremony, although it is fully aware that the theological dimension is absent. We must admit that there is also a conventional wedding, equally as anomalous as the conventional funeral. Here, too, the theological dimension is missing and the form of religiosity is substituted.

In anticipation of some of the problems which may well arise in seeking to eliminate the conventional funeral, we can point to several reasons for the persistence of the conventional wedding in spite of the clear choice between a religious and a civil ceremony. There is undoubtedly some magical assumption that a marriage will be happier if its beginning is blessed by a religious service, even though there is no personal commitment to the presuppositions of that service. There are also aesthetic reasons for preferring the conventional wedding, because the civil ritual has commonly been perfunctory and bleak. A judicial office hardly provides the setting for bridal gowns and aisle runners, candelabra and wedding marches. The inadequacy of such justifications for the conventional wedding should warn us that the mere offering of a choice between religious and humanistic funerals will not guarantee a thoughtful rejection of the conventional ceremony.

The proposal we make for a distinctive understanding and practice of Christian and humanistic funerals should not be misconstrued as a reaction of the church in pique to the frustrations of the struggle with secularism, nor is it a withdrawal of the church from the world because of impotence or irrelevance. The Christian church still regards all of mankind as subject to its concern. But at the same time it recognizes that it cannot with integrity force itself or its ministry upon those for whom it has no meaning.

A Theological Rationale for the Humanistic Funeral

The regard for differentiating religious and humanistic funerals presses us to clarify our understanding of the church. This proposal should not be regarded as a withdrawal from the world in the way which characterized Troeltsch's sect-type. This would be just as unsatisfactory as so completely embracing the world that there is no sense of identity for the church. The proposal we are making involves recognition of the needs of all men at a time of bereavement and seeks to meet those needs in ways which are relevant to the particular individual and capable of reception by him.

This, it would seem, is the largest, most comprehensive view of the church possible: to be so involved in the world that it is concerned for the needs of all men, seeking to provide for as many as it can, while at the same time encouraging all legitimate alternate means for satisfying the needs which the church cannot itself meet. Simply put, in the case of the funeral, the church is totally concerned for the needs of all who are bereaved. The church will seek to serve the needs of those who find the church's ministrations meaningful and helpful because their own faith and commitment makes them receptive. The church also acknowledges that there are those for whom its ministry would not be relevant or meaningful because they do not share in its faith and commitment. The church, out of concern for human need, will support such humanistic ministrations as will be received with meaning by the bereaved. Even though the church may not regard such ministrations as comprehensive, it nevertheless supports them. In this way it is seen that making provision for a humanistic funeral is a way in which the church actually broadens, not narrows, its concern.

While it would be extremely difficult for one who writes from the point of view of Protestant Christianity not to believe that the Christian funeral is more adequate and thus superior to the humanistic funeral, the reasons for this superiority should be understood. The Christian funeral is regarded as more adequate because it includes a dimension beyond the humanistic funeral. It bears witness to a relationship with God that places the whole experience in a different context. There is no sense in which this distinction is to imply a judgment upon the moral stature or personal worth either of the deceased or the bereaved. It is not a question of being judged good enough or not good enough to have a Christian funeral— for who can judge that? What is affirmed quite simply by this proposal is that the Christian funeral lacks its distinctive meaning when it is experienced by those who have neither conviction nor commitment as Christians. They will be best served by a ritual which bears the symbolic meanings that are most compatible with their view of life and death. Likewise, constant attention needs to be given to the Christian funeral to assure that it affords the best possible expression of Christian meanings for the bereaved.

143

7

Christian Meanings
in the Funeral

It is not enough to want to retain the funeral just because it is a time-honored custom. Any effort to suggest a constructive resolution of the tension between the funeral as a sterile anachronism and as an experience of value must be preceded by confronting certain crucial questions.

The Christian funeral is validated by the fact that it conveys distinctive Christian meanings. Foremost among these is the hope for the resurrection. All of the Christian meanings of the funeral rest on this single point. It is the means by which the Christian copes with death. It is the basis for the fellowship which sustains the bereaved. It is the foundation for the confident expectation that the mourner can be restored to a full life even after shattering personal tragedy.

The centrality of the resurrection in the Christian funeral points us to two questions: What is the place of the body in the Christian understanding of man? What is the meaning of the concept of resurrection in a modern scientific era? We cannot hope to support the value of a funeral without a detailed understanding of its most important meanings.

The Christian Meaning of the Body

What is the place of the body in the Christian understanding of man? This question has special meaning for the funeral

144

in several ways. One of the most commonly voiced objections to the funeral is that the body of the deceased is a major focus. The meaning of the body is involved in the rationale behind preservation of the corpse. The body of the deceased is very much bound up with the emotional reactions of the mourner.

We begin this consideration by acknowledging that there is a significant difference between the Greek philosophical understanding of man's nature and the Judeo-Christian understanding based upon the Old and New Testaments. At the same time it must be said that there has been such a consistent infusion of Greek thought into the Christian understanding, beginning in the early centuries of the Christian era, that a simple distinction between the two positions is quite difficult.

Platonic philosophy forms the basis for the dualistic understanding of man that became the foundation of the Greek view. Man is seen as divided into two distinct substances, a body and a soul. The soul is a portion of the divine essence which is placed into a material body. During life it remains a prisoner of the body, finding release only at the time of death. Because the soul is divine it is infinitely superior to the body. It is not amenable to the laws which govern matter but is subject to the divine law. When the soul is seen as the true spiritual essence of man, it is quite understandable that the purpose of life should be the cultivation of the soul and at the same time the suppression of all that is associated with the body. Death frees the immortal soul from its bodily prison and enables its escape to the pure spiritual realm of heaven. An excellent portrayal of this point of view is found in Plato's description of the death of Socrates in the Phaedo.

In contrast to the sublimity of the soul, the body is seen as a part of the material realm. In the dualistic philosophy this means that the body is associated with that which is base and evil. Greek thought, represented by Plato, was appreciative

145

of the beautiful and the good in the physical body, but these were always understood as the soul shining through the crude material matrix of the body. The body had only a temporary and subordinate place in man's nature.

The fact that these concepts do not seem very strange to our thinking indicates the degree to which the Greek mind has been instilled into Christian thought. This becomes all the more surprising when we confront the fact that the Judeo-Christian view as elaborated in the biblical understanding of man is diametrically opposed to such dualistic thought.

In this understanding there is no radical separation of spirit from matter, no understanding of a divine essence or immortal soul, no disparagement of the material body as a corporeal prison. As a part of God's creation the material world, including man's body, is not regarded as evil or worthless. As Justin Martyr wrote: "It is evident, therefore [from the Scriptures], that man made in the image of God was flesh. Is it not then absurd to say that the flesh made by God in his own image is contemptible and worth nothing? But that the flesh is with God a precious possession is manifest first from its being formed by him." [1] This stubborn resistance to the anti-materialism of Greek ideas has remained a persistent theme in Christian thought even though it has often escaped the popular mind.

The biblical understanding, as we shall shortly describe it in detail, resists any effort to divide the nature of man into discrete component parts. It always regards man as a whole, a totality, a psychosomatic unity. So thoroughgoing was this unitary understanding that any reference to a "part" of man's nature was always taken to represent the "whole" of man. The Hebrews could speak of man's "heart" or his "flesh" as representative of the total man. The Old Testament in Hebrew

---

[1] Justin Martyr, "On the Resurrection," quoted in D. R. G. Owen, *Body and Soul* (Philadelphia: Westminster Press, 1956), p. 53.

does not even have a word that can be translated "body" in the sense in which we use it to describe the whole structure of flesh and bones. The eleven Hebrew words for what we regard as parts or aspects of man which were eventually rendered as "body" in the Septuagint and subsequent translations are so fully imbued with the concept of totality that any separate word to describe the whole is unnecessary.

This theme of psychosomatic unity is replacing many of the dualistic presuppositions of the Greek mind in a good deal of the theory and practice of modern medicine and psychiatry. Even though the context for understanding man may be humanistic, there is a real departure from crude materiality and isolated psychic faculties. Contemporary medical research and practice involves the psychic causes and consequences of physical dysfunction. Contemporary psychiatry, for example the work of Erik Erikson, sees the human personality developing out of three thoroughly interpenetrating, interdependent processes: the somatic process, the social process, and the ego process. In such scientific disciplines there is growing recognition that man can be adequately regarded only as a whole, a totality.

New Testament Foundations

In the New Testament, although the Greek language provided words for flesh, body, soul, and spirit, these words were used with the strong Hebraic accent on unity and wholeness. It is at this point that we must be most careful in our effort to understand the biblical view of man. If we use the words naïvely and uncritically, we can easily fall into the not uncommon mixture of Greek dualism. If we would be true to the original understanding, we must preserve the context of wholeness and totality.

One of the commonly used New Testament words is *sarx,*

regularly translated as flesh.[2] Occasionally this term is applied to actual tissue; man's flesh and animal's meat. But more often, when applied to man, it is not thought of as that part of man which we call fleshy tissue but as the total man understood in terms of his physical existence. In this respect it is much like our common reference to our children as "our own flesh and blood." Sarx is also used to describe man in his distance from God. It refers to mortal man, man in a state of separation from God. As such he is a part of the whole creation which is alienated from the Creator. Again it must be noted that this is not a form of the dualistic idea that the material aspect of man's nature is evil. It is rather the whole man apart from God that is regarded as flesh. Perhaps this is best illustrated by observing that the list of "works of the flesh" in Galatians 5 contains only a few sections involving the physical body, such as sexual immorality, drunkenness, carousing; and a majority of nonphysical attitudes, such as enmity, jealousy, selfishness, envy. Sarx (flesh) then refers not so much to the mass of tissue that is a part of man as it does to the whole man in his natural state of alienation from God.

A second Greek word which relates to this understanding of man is soma, which is translated as body.[3] Soma normally includes everything we have said about sarx and then proceeds further. We, under the subtle influence of Greek thought, commonly think of man as having a body as if that body were a portion of the total man, as opposed to other portions, mind or spirit. Biblical thought with its assumption of a psychosomatic unity would say with Robinson that man is a body. In a sense it is very similar to the theme of contemporary psychology that man does not have a personality as a part of his being but rather that a man's being is his personality. Indeed, it has often been held that our modern concept of personality,

[2] For more detailed explanation see John A. T. Robinson, *The Body* (London: SCM Press, 1952), pp. 17-26.
[3] *Ibid.*, pp. 26-33.

seen in its fullest meaning as the whole of man, the self, is an extremely adequate translation for *soma* (body).

The meaning of *soma* diverges from the meaning of *sarx* particularly when seen in the context of man's relationship to God. *Sarx* (flesh) indicates the whole man in a condition of alienation from God, while *soma* (body) represents the whole man intended for relationship with God. In the New Testament context *sarx* tends toward mortality and destruction, *soma* toward a hoped-for restoration of relationship with God.

A third biblical concept figuring in this discussion is *pneuma* (spirit). Again the pattern of psychosomatic unity needs to be applied. The biblical concept of spirit is not to be understood in the format of Greek thought as the nonmaterial, that part of man which inhabits his body, or even the essence of man. The Hebrew view which underlies both the Old and New Testaments would find the concept of a separable spiritual portion of man quite foreign. A disembodied spirit would be an anomaly because it would represent the impossible dissolution of the psychomatic unity which is man.

In the New Testament, particularly the writings of Paul, there is frequent opposition of the concepts flesh and spirit. Because of the persistence of Greek thinking in the modern mind it is easy to misunderstand the meaning of this opposition. It is not as if two portions of man's being were opposed to each other, as in the case of the Greek dualism of body and soul. Rather, Paul refers to two opposing qualities of relationship with God. Flesh here represents the whole man as separated from and opposed to God, while spirit represents the whole man in a relationship of love with God and fellowman.[4] The word *pneuma* then describes a stance, a pattern of organization of the total man.

Finally, there is the concept *psyche* (soul). In the Pauline letters of the New Testament it is used to translate the Hebrew

[4] Cf. D. R. G. Owen, *Body and Soul*, pp. 192 f.

149

nephesh, which is the self, the whole person, the living being. Rather than being a fragment of the divine essence, as the Greek would define it, it again represents a perspectival view of the total man.

It is further evidence of the wholistic understanding that the New Testament is able to speak of a *soma pneumatikon* (a spiritual body) and a *soma tes sarkos* (a body of the flesh), but there is no combination of flesh and spirit, no fleshly spirit. This is not because, as the Greeks would say, matter and spirit are mutually exclusive. Rather it is because total man seen as alienated from God is separated by definition from total man in relationship with God. In either instance the whole man is involved.

Death and the Whole Man

We need to ponder the effect of death upon man seen in these various aspects. The Greeks would see death as release of the immortal spirit from the mortal body. This idea has thoroughly imbued a great deal of Christian thought. Death is then misunderstood as a boon, a relief, a gateway to higher existence, rather than as a destructive antagonist. The biblical understanding is that just as life involves the total man, so does death. There is no immortal part of man, no section of man's being that does not die. Death is not seen as a dividing of man into component parts, some of which perish while others survive. All of man's being dies. No part of his being by nature remains tied to life.

If this biblical theme of understanding man both in life and in death as a totality is taken seriously, what does it have to say to some of the issues raised in discussion of the funeral? The most obvious of these is the often expressed concern that any emphasis upon the body of the deceased should be resisted because it is felt that it de-emphasizes or detracts from the spiritual. This resistance has taken the form of opposition

150

to viewing the corpse, to preparation of the body for viewing, to having the body present at the funeral. The corpse is regarded as the material, mortal portion of the person from which the immaterial soul has been freed to live on in eternity. Because of this clear-cut division, it is felt that anything which pays attention to the body diverts attention from the spirit.

If the biblical frame of reference of man as psychosomatic unity is accepted, the concern just described is no real issue. Any separation of body and spirit is impossible, any separation of flesh (understood as substance, tissue) from spirit is inconceivable. The Judeo-Christian understanding does not think of a spirit flying out of the body at the time of death. Death is total. Everything about the person is dead.

We have to ponder the relationship of the corpse of the deceased to his body (understood as the whole man) in life. One's sense of his body is very much tied to selfhood. Gordon Allport gives us a rather crude illustration of this fact.[5] He points out that the salivary glands are constantly secreting within our mouths, and we are constantly swallowing the saliva which they have produced. But if we were to imagine expectorating several times into a glass and then drinking the saliva which was only recently in our mouths, we would find it most repulsive. The point is that so long as a substance does not leave the body it is a part of us, but if it gets outside the body it is no longer seen as a part of the self and is regarded as a foreign substance. In life the body is inextricably tied to the self.

If we think of the body in life in terms of the external presence of the whole man, is there not a sense in which the body remains the external presence of the whole man following death? This is not to deny that it is a dead body, nor that the whole man is dead. It is not a matter of seeking to imply that a corpse is imperishable, for at this point all of

[5] *Pattern and Growth in Personality* (New York: Holt, Rinehart & Winston, 1961), p. 114.

man is perishable. Obviously the dissolution of the external presence of a man follows death rather quickly, but this does not mean that all the rest of man is not dead too. Man is no less a totality in death than he is in life.

Actually, the tension we are dealing with is not so much the tension between flesh and body, sarx and soma. Even here it might be falsely assumed that the body (defined as personality) survives while the flesh is separated from it and perishes. This would again be the Greek way of thinking of the body as the form and the flesh as the substance of which the body is made. The biblical view does not think in these terms but sees the only separation of flesh and body as two perspectives on man—man separated from God and man made for potential relationship with God. The corpse of the deceased in a very real sense represents both perspectives.

The Funeral and the Whole Man

Thus we ask: Is not the corpse of the deceased one of the legitimate focuses of the funeral? Certainly it is not the only focus, nor even the primary focus, for the mourners and their needs are of utmost importance. Nevertheless, this wholistic understanding of man strongly suggests that the body of the dead is appropriately one of the significant elements of the funeral. The corpse is not to be looked upon as mere matter, base, impure, of absolutely no consequence. If this were true then it would be quite legitimate to want to be rid of it as soon as possible, to view it as rubbish to be disposed of quickly. The dualistic Greek understanding easily lends itself to this.

It is interesting to note a difference between the attitudes of Roman Catholic priests and Protestant ministers toward the body as reported by Fulton.[6] Roman Catholics acknowledge

[6] Robert L. Fulton, "The Clergyman and the Funeral Director: A Study in Role Conflict," *Social Forces*, XXXVII (1961), 317-23.

the funeral as a way of honoring both the memory and the body of the deceased. They stress the importance of the body as a temple of the Holy Spirit and, as such, worthy of respect and consideration in life and in death. Protestant clergymen accord little positive value to the body but give virtually their sole attention to the mourners, feeling that the funeral has to do only with the living. Both of these viewpoints are fundamentally Greek. The Roman Catholic position represents the Aristotelianism blended into Roman dogma by Thomas Aquinas, in which the physical body is important because it it included in man's ultimate redemption, with the body regarded as the matter of the soul and the soul as the form of the body. The Protestant position described could well represent the Platonic understanding in which death released the soul from the body, so the important thing is to make possible the cultivation, or at least the exaltation, of the soul. Neither of these views reflects the biblical understanding in which the dead body is the representation of the dead totality.

This is not a matter of trying to hold on to the deceased by focusing on his corpse. It must be recognized as a dead body. There is no effort at illusion of life warranted here. It is the death of the whole person that is being represented. The corpse represents the external presence, not of the living nor the partially alive, but of the dead.

The basic Hebrew-Christian understanding of the whole man, living or dead, also counteracts the tendency to seek to keep death separate from life. That separation, as we have seen in an earlier chapter, is based upon the maintenance of an illusion. Death in the biblical view is so radical that it sweeps away any illusion. It is a hard, inescapable fact. This death is not partial, nor is it a welcome release into pure life. It is an illusion that only the material which has been the matrix of the spirit dies, while the real being lives on. Dualism enables death to be seen as cut off from the real essence of the person, which it cannot touch, and thus from life. The

153

biblical view sees death as total. It has to be faced in life for what it is, for avoidance is truly impossible.

The Resurrection of the Body

The concept of the resurrection of the body has been a part of the Christian understanding of life and death and life after death from the beginning of the church. Since a sizable proportion of pastors queried defined the funeral as a witness to the hope for resurrection, this doctrine of the church has important implications for the funeral.

The concept of resurrection poses problems in different ways for different persons. For the secularist resurrection has been a meaningless idea. His empirically oriented view of life sees it in terms of flux and perishability. His understanding of reality provides no reasonable basis for assuming any kind of existence after death. All animate things, including man, pass through the cycle of life from birth to death. Having run their course they dissolve into the elements of nature from whence they came.

Christians through the centuries have had problems of another sort regarding the resurrection. Detours into dualistic understandings which substitute the concept of immortality of the soul for that of resurrection of the body have been persistent. This position envisions the spiritual essence of man as separable from the nonessential body. The spirit involves all that is high and good; while the body, as a part of the material world, is inferior, perishable, a necessary evil. So pronounced is the cleavage between the spiritual and the material that the very notion of resurrection of the body seems monstrous and anomalous. This position was advanced in the early period of the church by Gnosticism, Neoplatonism, and Manichaeism, and in each instance was resisted as thoroughly inconsistent with the New Testament view.

The biblical view of totality deals with life and death and

154

new life after death in terms of the total death of man and the restoration of all of his being. The Christian sees that man lives as a *whole*, dies as a *whole*, and is given new life as a *whole* man.

This concept of the totality of man's nature has been applied to the Christian understanding of resurrection in a number of ways. Dahl [7] describes the traditional centuries-old view as a belief that resurrection constituted a restoration and miraculous improvement of the present physical body, a literal reconstruction of the body, even though it may have deteriorated after death. This concept is strikingly similar to the belief in resurrection as held by the Pharisees in New Testament times. Their expectation was that the physical body would be restored to life to such an extent that even the defects of the body would be perpetuated. There is evidence that Paul was resisting this notion of restoration of the physical body with his assertion that flesh and blood cannot inherit the kingdom of God (I Cor. 15:50). There is also a refined dualism implied in this traditional view because here resurrection brings about a reuniting of body and spirit, which are regarded as having been estranged since man's fall.

Dahl then proceeds to point to a newer position which rejects the literalism and materialism of the traditional position in favor of acknowledging the dissolution of the present body and the giving of another, a new body, in the resurrection. Radical discontinuity, total change, is a chief characteristic of this viewpoint. This understanding shares some of the features of reincarnation—the ending of one life and the completely new beginning of another. Again problems are forthcoming because if a totally new body is involved in resurrection, the implication is that some nonphysical essence persists to continue the personal identity of the individual. This would

[7] M. E. Dahl, *The Resurrection of the Body* (Naperville: Alec R. Allenson, 1962), pp. 7-10.

again necessitate a separation within man's nature which is inconsistent with the biblical understanding of wholeness.

A third position advanced by Dahl is somatic identity. In this position he seeks to preserve both the radical discontinuity and the radical continuity with which the New Testament views death and resurrection. This he does by rejecting the concept of material identity (as held by the traditional view) and the concept of total newness (as held by the another-body view) in favor of what he calls somatic identity. He explains this identity with a very interesting illustration:

"Body" in St. Paul means the whole personality, and resurrection means the restoration—the final salvation—of that unified personality. Hence it is vital to insist on the word *identity* as describing this relationship, because the whole idea has no meaning unless it is the *same* personality that is to be raised that exists now. Many of the misunderstandings of this . . . stem from the tendency to think of this as a *material* identity. If I say, this gold ring is the *same* ring I lost three years ago, I mean that it is composed of the same lump of gold, the same atoms, as the ring I lost. But if I say, this is the *same man* I met in London seven years ago, I mean he is the *same person* (in Pauline terms the same "body"), knowing that the particular cells of his "body" (in the modern sense) have completely changed since then. This identity is not simply a matter of his having the same "personality" (conceived of in the modern sense, i.e. of a nonmaterial something-or-other *in* a "body"), nor simply a matter of his having the same thoughts, memories, associations, character, etc., but also of having the same "body" (in the modern sense).[8]

In this fashion it is possible to affirm the unitary nature of man in a way which accepts the possibility of significant changes without requiring only radical discontinuity. Death does destroy the whole man and the resurrection brings new life to the whole man. This new life, insofar as the New Testa-

[8] *Ibid.*, p. 94

ment describes it, is neither an exact reproduction of the present life (a restoration) nor the complete abrogation of the present life (a totally new and utterly different identity).

The whole matter of continuity and discontinuity is dealt with in Paul's metaphor of the seed and the plant (I Cor. 15:36 ff). The actual substance of the seed deteriorates; nevertheless, the new plant comes from the seed. The old is made new. There is an element of continuity to be sure, but there is also change of a most radical nature.

So often the infusion of Greek dualism has supported the assumption that the resurrection overcomes the crude materiality of the body and successfully creates a kind of totally spiritual existence. It was this kind of mistaken notion against which the formulators of earlier creedal statements were reacting when they propounded the phrase "the resurrection of the flesh," which is the original Greek phrasing of the Apostles' Creed. Although this phrase and the literalization of this concept are nonbiblical, the effort was being made to counteract the spiritualization of the resurrection by the dualists and the Docetists. Yet any understanding of this phrase which would indicate the resurrection of the flesh as substance stands in direct contradiction to the great Pauline treatise on the resurrection in I Corinthians 15.

Here the several meanings of flesh (sarx) which have been described earlier are of help to us. Sarx understood as tissue certainly deteriorates after death. Sarx, in its other sense, as the whole man in a state of alienation from God, if it continues, eventuates in nothing. This is true not because it is flesh-substance, or matter, but because it is separated from God.

The resurrection in the New Testament understanding is not so much the making or remaking of a new substance as it is the creation of a new relationship with God. The resurrection of the body (soma) is the giving of new life to the whole man considered as one meant to be in relationship with God.

According to the Christian understanding, this resurrection is affirmed by the resurrection of Jesus Christ. The faith of the church is that Jesus Christ rose from the dead following his death on the cross, that he is a living Christ. The Pauline figure, describing the church as the body of Christ, establishes the tie between the resurrected Christ and his followers. As the individual Christian becomes a member of the body of Christ, he begins to participate in the resurrection. His whole being, his soma, is being transformed daily as more and more he is fulfilled in deepening relationship with God in Christ. The body of Christ is understood as a corporate personality in which each member becomes the self which he can become only in relationship to God.

Some, like John A. T. Robinson and Rudolf Bultmann,[9] understand resurrection mainly in this way. It has primarily to do with the quality of the life of the Christian in relationship to God now.

Others see the life-giving activity of the Holy Spirit now present in the whole person of the Christian as beginning the process of new life which in a sense is the precursor of life after death. The Christian faith gives assurance of resurrection by the provision of present new life, but the Christian still confronts the reality of physical death as a part of the natural order of things. He is transformed in the present life, but he remains a mortal, dying man. His death is no illusion. His whole being is annihilated to receive new life after death.

Oscar Cullmann cautions us against a purely spiritualized conception of this new life, both in the present and the future. Assuming the New Testament understanding of the wholistic nature of man, he points out that the resurrection has a present effect upon the whole man, including his physical body. The

[9] John A. T. Robinson, The Body; Rudolf Bultmann, "New Testament and Mythology," Kerygma and Myth, ed. by Hans W. Bartsch, trans. by Reginald Fuller (London: S.P.C.K. Press, 1953), I, 1-44.

way in which the whole person is involved is illustrated by Cullmann's point:

All Paul's teaching on sexual morality is bound up with the idea of the body of Christ. This idea explains his reason for upholding the sanctity of marriage. It is that marriage is the only sexual union between two bodies which is compatible with union with the body of Christ. . . . We arrive, then, at the conclusion that in the New Testament the resurrection of Christ has consequences for our bodies.[10]

The significant question posed here is this: If relationship to the risen Christ now affects our bodies (i.e., our whole selves including our physical bodies), is there not justification for holding that this is also true at the time of death? It would seem that the Christian affirmation that death has been overcome in the resurrection of Christ would mean that the effect of that resurrection on the whole person of the Christian would not be less in death than it is in life. It would not have to do with a fragment of the person, a spirit detached from the material, but with the entire being of the person.

Myth and the Modern Mind

To this point we have been examining the concept of the resurrection largely through the eyes of the person who accepts its reality. At the same time it must be frankly recognized that this concept is not meaningful for many persons.

The scientifically oriented man of the twentieth century is basically a monist. He rejects dualism, just as does classical Christianity, but for a different reason. Instead of affirming in the largest possible sense man as a psychosomatic unity, he sees man as a unity of mind and body. However, mind is so closely related to body function that consciousness is regarded

[10] *The Early Church* (London: SCM Press, 1956), p. 173.

as a product of physical function alone. All of man's nature is thus reduced to the material dimension. In this point of view man does not differ essentially from the higher animals. He may have reached a higher level of development, but there are no transcendent elements in him which differentiate him from other living things. This position regards material reality as the only reality. Since death is obviously the conclusion of natural existence, its finality is regarded as absolute. The death of every man is just as conclusive and terminal as the death of a pet animal or a tree. The lack of empirical evidence causes the scientific mind to reject any concept of resurrection. The language and thought forms in which this article of faith has been couched through the centuries appear to many persons obsolete and irrelevant.

Christian theology has not been unaware of the plight of the scientifically oriented mind. Leading the theological grappling with this problem has been Rudolf Bultmann. Sensing the difficulty of the twentieth-century intellect in pressing meaning from the mythological thought forms of past centuries, Bultmann has sought a solution in a method he calls demythologizing. Myths of the past have been endeavors to describe the action of powers of another world upon this world. However, since myths have their origin in a prescientific era, they are no longer intelligible to the scientific mind. "The real purpose of myth is not to present an objective picture of the world as it is, but to express man's understanding of himself in the world in which he lives. Myth should be interpreted not cosmologically, but anthropologically, or better still, existentially." [11] A myth, then, must be used to help a person to interpret the real meaning of his life.

The resurrection of Jesus Christ, upon which Christians have rested their hope in the resurrection, is, according to Bultmann, one of the major myths of the New Testament. He

[11] "New Testament and Mythology," *Kerygma and Myth*, p. 10.

senses the difficulty that the scientific mind has in accepting the New Testament accounts of the resurrection. He resolves the problem by discounting the historicity of these events. The only thing about the New Testament accounts that is certain is that the early church asserted its faith in the resurrection. But, from Bultmann's position, whether or not the events of the first Easter are historical or not is not the real question. What needs to be asked is, What does the myth of the resurrection mean to the living of any century? The real purpose of the myth of the resurrection is described in this way: "Only as it stimulates him [the Christian] to newness of life does it have personal and ultimate significance. Precisely this is what it does. One is raised with Christ so that he knows a resurrection of his true life in the present hour in that he lives now for God and not for self." [12]

The importance of the resurrection accounts in the New Testament, for Bultmann, is what meaning was produced by them in the lives of the disciples. In the present time, quite apart from any concern for whether or not the resurrection of Jesus Christ is historical, the importance of the resurrection is the way in which man is moved to find his true existence by being dependent upon God rather than by seeking security in his own resources. The meaning beneath the myth of the resurrection is that God is worthy of trust and that complete trust in him brings man to authentic existence.

Resurrection, according to this position, has little to do with the standard assumptions about life after death. It is concerned for the production of a quality of true existence in the present. As such it provides a means for coping with the fear of death. Bultmann follows the theme of existentialism which holds that the honest confrontation of death and the apprehending of authentic existence are bound together. True existence here would mean a life thoroughly involved in a faith-full relation-

[12] George W. Davis, *Existentialism and Theology* (New York: Philosophical Library, 1957), p. 56.

ship with God. The resurrection, demythologized, has as its primary purpose the production and enabling of such faith.

This is not the place to become caught up in the intense debate which has evolved between Bultmann and his critics. For our purposes it is sufficient to indicate that even in this radical reappraisal of the meaning of resurrection there is an emphasis upon new life. The future dimension of this new life is eclipsed by its present reality, but the concept of newness nevertheless persists.

No matter what theological interpretation of the resurrection one finds most meaningful, the issue finally distills to a matter of faith. Lacking the kinds of proof which scientific investigation requires, the Christian can only affirm his own confidence in the meaningfulness of resurrection. He has to decide on the basis of personal commitment rather than objective verification where the ultimate answer really rests. Granted that modern man's capacity to tolerate mystery is considerably strained at this point, he can neither fully penetrate the veil which hides both past and future from the present nor can he fully deprecate the meaning of these dimensions because they are not totally comprehensible. The only basis upon which his apprehension of the meaning of resurrection can rest is his confidence that while the finality of death looms large in man's view, for God death is not ultimately final.

The Resurrection and the Funeral

Against the background of this discussion of the theological understanding of resurrection we now seek its implications for the funeral.

First of all, we see that the resurrection concept makes the differentiation of the Christian funeral and the humanistic funeral necessary. There need be no effort to apply this differentiation in a judgmental sense, using it to indicate superiority or inferiority. This is a matter of objective definition. The Christian funeral is lacking in meaning without the confidence in resurrection, and the humanistic funeral has no meaningful place for it.

If persons are unable to share in the meaning of hope for resurrection, the Christian funeral is lacking in significance for them. Thus some of the primary meanings which this ritual seeks to convey find no basis for relevant reception. The humanistic funeral, as we shall see in the next chapter, will provide a response for many of their needs in a way that is more meaningful for them.

The Christian funeral is integrally tied to the concept of resurrection. The hope for new life is the foundation for the coping function of the Christian funeral. This hope enables the Christian to confront death without denying the reality of its destructive force. He need not seek to separate life from death but can bring them into dynamic confrontation. He is certain of the power of death over life, but he is also confident of the power of new life over death.

The Christian funeral, then, can be totally realistic in its presentation of death. There is no need for illusion or concealment. Death can be acknowledged as bringing finality to present relationships as they have been known, while positing the possibility of a new quality of relationship. Death is recognized as both a necessary and an inevitable prelude to resurrection.

At the same time the present form of new life, acknowledged as a deepening relationship with God in this existence as well as an anticipation of new life to come, prevents the Christian from courting death. He need not rush toward death in order to escape from the limitations of this life. Since the Christian can confront death without either dreadful anxiety or passionate longing because of his hope for resurrection, he is able to face both life and death with poise and equanimity. The confidence in resurrection makes possible the same poise in the

Christian funeral. For the Christian it is certainly marked by sadness because of separation, but it is not an experience which marks total, ultimate annihilation of the person. By the same token it is not an occasion for unalloyed joy because even resurrection is preceded by very real death.

We have already commented in some detail on the effect of the wholistic understanding of man's nature on the funeral. Since the concept of resurrection is set squarely upon this view of man as totality, we can make the same assertions here. This concept does introduce some new dimensions to our consideration. Among these is the theme of continuity and discontinuity which is a part of biblical understanding of resurrection.

This theme has particular reference to the place which the body of the deceased often plays in the funeral ritual. Assuming that the New Testament is correct in pointing out that man is really a totality rather than a composite of separable parts, the place of the body in the funeral is affected. This is not to say that belief in the resurrection of the whole man dictates any particular practice involving the body, but it does most certainly shape attitudes toward the body, the corpse of the deceased.

Even some of the more traditional forms of the concept of resurrection have been implicitly dualistic. As we have already seen, a popular notion among Christians has been that body and soul separated at the time of death, the spirit lived on while the body perished, then the immortal spirit and the resurrected body were rejoined at the end of time. This belief can have one of two effects upon the way in which the body is regarded. On the one hand, because it is seen as the perishable part of the person it can be disregarded and virtually ignored. This attitude is commonly held in Protestant churches. On the other hand, if this body will someday be raised from the grave, it must be highly regarded. Thus, for example, one finds the Roman Catholic Church resisting cremation because it is an unnatural form of dissolution which is not regarded as proper for the body of a Christian.

If, however, one accepts the biblical position that the resurrection involves the whole man, a new perspective emerges. That which we call man's body is no less a part of him than that which we call his spirit. Death touches radically the total man, so that one part cannot be lightly discarded while another is brought to its fulfillment. There are those who have felt that minimal attention given to the body of the deceased enhanced the spiritual aspect of his nature and therefore was proper Christian perspective. But we must ask if the New Testament understanding of resurrection, with its elements of continuity and discontinuity cutting across the totality of man's being, does not call this assumption into question. If death brings total annihilation to all of man's being, and if the concept of man as a whole is taken seriously, can we assume that the body of the deceased is any less a part of him than his spirit? In fact, from our human perspective, one needs to question earnestly whether or not the body, by virtue of its tangible presence before the funeral, is not a proper and adequate representation of the person, so long as it is fully and realistically acknowledged that he is dead.

The tension between continuity and discontinuity that the concept of resurrection contains also has implications for the preservation of the body. The element of discontinuity certainly indicates that the concept of resurrection provides no warrant for the long-term preservation of the body. There is no Christian basis for practices similar to those of the Egyptians, who sought to preserve and reanimate the body in order to assure its survival beyond death. To assume that embalming or shielding the corpse from the elements is in any way connected with the hope for resurrection lacks foundation.

At the same time, although it should not be asserted that the concept of resurrection demands it, the theme of continuity provides some rationale for the short-term preservation of the corpse as an intermediate stage in the separation process. Totally to ignore or even to depreciate the body, the medium through which the individual has been known, may well be an ignoring of the element of continuity. This is not to say that the actual dead physical body is the continuing factor. This is not the case, for the corpse is already involved in the process of dissolution. But, in spite of its transient nature, even its temporary presence after death can symbolize the conviction that somatic identity (cf. p. 156) is reestablished and that there is a sense in which the continuity of personhood pertains in the resurrection.

Two thousand years of theological reflection have made the resurrection no less a mystery than it was in the first century of our era. Yet it has persisted as one of the central meanings of the Christian faith enabling the confrontation with death. The unique quality of the Christian funeral rests on this meaning.

8

New Designs for
the Funeral

One of the canons of contemporary design is that form follows function. Design must, therefore, be related to usefulness and efficiency. But even more, design seeks to integrate usefulness and beauty. The designer's problem is to find forms which meet diverse and complicated needs. This dictum does not mean that practicality is the only consideration, but it does compel us to look for a purposefulness in all design. Furthermore, recognizing that rarely is an object limited to one function, certain judgments have to be made regarding which functions are most significant and thus have the most right to influence form.

Our search for new designs for the funeral has to take into account a number of functions that the funeral serves, pointed to in earlier chapters. Criteria for evaluating effective function have also been described. These, too, become a part of establishing designs for the funeral.

Several assumptions are basic to our effort to lay out new designs for the funeral. First, the rationale of the funeral is fundamentally sound. The psychological, social, and theological principles for helping those who are bereaved are well enough established to enable us to describe with some adequacy the function of the funeral. This ritual, rightly understood and conducted, has the potentiality for providing the form by which these functions are fulfilled.

Second, over the years some forms have developed which

have not been related to the major purposes of the funeral or which may reflect minor functions that disregard or even counteract more significant functions. An example of this displacement of major function by one far less important is seen in the way in which seeking the long-term preservation of the body tends to cancel out the work of affirming the finality that is involved in death.

Third, the existence of forms which do not follow the real function of the funeral has only damaged, but has not destroyed, the validity of the funeral. This book does not share the view of some that the funeral is anachronistic and obsolete or that it is so perverted from its original function that it is suitable only for discard. We shall seek to show that it is possible to foresee a reclamation of full value in the funeral by reuniting function and form.

Thus, our goal here is a design for the funeral which is not dedicated to the status quo but which seeks to preserve or restyle those elements that can be demonstrated to be consistent with the function of the funeral as a valuable means for helping the mourners.

The Response to Pluralism

The major, and possibly most far-reaching, proposal for new design involves a clear differential definition of the religious and the humanistic funeral. This proposal is a response to the pluralistic situation in our society. Only about 60 percent of our population are affiliated with any church or synagogue. This would mean that nearly half of those who suffer bereavement take part in funeral rites which convey values that are not shared by them and are not meaningfully received.

It is perfectly justifiable to define the Christian funeral as a religious service, but to insist that all funerals are religious services is to ignore the nontheological norms for the funeral. This would be no more responsible than to suggest the complete secularization of the funeral, for this would deny the validity of the theological criteria even for religious persons. Still another possible position would suggest that the present practice of conducting conventional (pseudoreligious) funerals be continued, assuming that those without religious conviction would disregard the theological elements of the funeral which seem irrelevant to them but would still profit from the social and psychological features of the funeral. Perhaps this is so, but it poses real difficulties. Elements of hypocrisy in such a pattern can easily make the whole service seem empty of meaning. The conventional funeral in many ways works against the mourning process because it is patently only an appearance, alienated from reality.

Our proposal for a clear understanding of religious and humanistic funerals would do away with what has been described as the conventional funeral. Honest alternatives are available which can provide the best possible help in bereavement. A mourning family has a clear choice to be made on the basis of the kind of funeral from which they will receive fuller meaning. The pastor and the funeral director can offer meaningful options which violate neither the integrity of the family nor that of the church.

Now let us examine in more detail first the design of the religious funeral and then the humanistic design. A decade ago I wrote that the proper function of the church is either to revive the true meanings of the present pattern of the funeral consistent with the Christian interpretations of death and mourning or to invent new patterns which are relevant to the actual situation. This task is still crucial and involves both the religious and the humanistic funerals.

The Religious Funeral

Again, it must be pointed out that this study is written from the point of view of Protestant Christianity. The task of interpreting the religious funeral for other Christian and non-Christian faith communities is not attempted here but remains to be carried out from within those faiths.

The Christian funeral can fulfill a number of valid functions which in turn should influence the form of the funeral.

SUPPORTIVE RELATIONSHIPS

The Christian funeral has as one of its functions the provision of a framework of supportive relationship. This relationship is two-dimensional. On the one hand, the Christian funeral manifests a relatedness between God and the mourners. There is a sense in which God is involved in their suffering. Neither life nor death, the living or the dead, are beyond the scope of his concern. On the other hand, the Christian funeral demonstrates a relatedness between the bereaved and a community which shares his loss. Within this community, he gains support for undergoing the difficult and painful experience of mourning.

The form of the Christian funeral which follows the function of providing a framework of supportive relationship is that of a worship service of the church. Here both dimensions of the relational context are made clear. Worship is representative of the God-man relationship. Since it is the worship of the church, it also involves a worshiping congregation of which the mourners are a part.

Worship implies an object of devotion. In the setting of the Christian funeral there is acknowledgment of the providence of God. This does not mean, as it is sometimes stated, that the Christian needs to accept with forbearance the loss he has suffered as a "gift" of God's providence. Nor does it mean that death is an arbitrary act of God's will. Yet, because life and death are not separated, God's providence can be seen a part of each. God's loving care and merciful concern are extended to the living and the dead.

God's care, expressed in relationship, becomes a resource to

170

enable widening hope and deepening trust. The mourner knows that the providence of God encompasses the loved one who has died as well as the mourner who has suffered loss. This providence is expressed in the doctrine of the resurrection which is the heart of the Christian funeral. God gives new life to the deceased and also to those whose whole existence now requires a new orientation.

The form of the funeral as worship does not constitute the relationship with God but rather affirms its existence as a resource for facing life and death in the context of that relationship.

The horizontal dimension of worship, the relationship of person to person, is also a part of the form of the funeral. A congregation, a community of the faithful, is involved in a two-way relationship—with God and with one another. This is not just an observing community, but one which actually participates. In this corporate experience there is a tangible affirmation that death has affected the entire group. All have in some respect suffered loss. The group itself has actually been touched and changed by death.

Since bereavement is a shared experience, the group stands ready to support each of its members, particularly those who are most deeply involved in this individual loss. One of the ways in which the group fulfills this function is by just standing by to sustain the mourners until they have sufficient strength to assimilate their loss. Another way is through a corporate expression of the meanings which are carriers of their confidence and hope. Individual mourners are sustained by the group expression and acceptance of these meanings. This becomes a kind of assurance that their deepest hopes are not merely private wishful thinking.

The new design for the Christian funeral will seek to make the worship form more adequate for fulfilling the function of providing supportive relationship by enabling maximum participation in the funeral by the community of faith. This means

171

that the funeral should be so arranged that a maximum number of the community can be present and participating, a theme we shall speak of later. It also means that the worship itself should involve the worshipers as participants rather than observers. In some liturgical traditions this will be more easily done than in others. In all, however, there is the possibility for actual group participation in the singing of appropriate hymns, the praying of prayers in unison, the recitation of one of the historic creeds or a congregational statement of faith, or even periods of guided silent prayer. Too much the funeral has become a service read by a pastor while a congregation looks on passively. A new design intended to restore important meaning to the funeral will seek to enable maximum participation.

CHRISTIAN MEANINGS

A second major function of the Christian funeral grows out of the recognition that it is a ritual intended to convey Christian meaning regarding life and death. This meaning is presented within a context of faith. As we have seen, this includes a relationship with the object of faith, God, and relationship with a community of faith, the church. Within the context of this dual relationship death is seen in close conjunction with life. Dying is given meaning as a part of life. The function of the funeral is to provide a structure of meaning into which death can be fitted. From the Christian viewpoint this involves providing the resource of a trusting relationship with God as the bereaved faces two great tasks: the assimilation of the reality of the death of a loved one into the meaning of present life and the strengthening of the mourner to cope with the fact of his own death. The meaning which is found in his relationship with God helps man to place his experience into a context much larger than his own life. The Christian faith enables this confrontation of death and dying because of confidence in God's gift of new life.

The second mode in which the form of the Christian funeral is to follow its function is seen in the ways in which Christian meanings are conveyed both in the formal ritual of the funeral and in related practices. The meanings of which we speak here are related to the understanding of life and death, to the understanding of how death changes one's relationship with the deceased, to the way in which bereavement causes one to reflect on his own mortality and on the meaning of his own life.

The passages of scripture which are read at the Christian funeral service are an effective avenue for carrying the meanings of the entire heritage of the Christian faith. Here a person can find the assurance that the great issues posed by death have been confronted before and that the faith speaks to these issues.

If we examine the scripture passages which are most commonly found in various orders for the burial of the dead, we see that there are several pervasive meanings which can speak to the situation of mourning as we have described it. A major emphasis is placed on assurances of God's care extended in both life and death. The Christian position that life and death are not to be separated but are to be seen together is conveyed in such passages as these: "If we live, we live to the Lord, and if we die, we die to the Lord; so then, whether we live or whether we die, we are the Lord's" (Rom. 14:8); or, "For I am sure that neither death, nor life . . . will be able to separate us from the love of God in Christ Jesus our Lord" (Rom. 8:38-39).

The meanings that speak to the way in which death affects the relationship between the mourners and the deceased are primarily contained in the theme of resurrection. This is the Christian confidence in the gift of new life provided by the goodness of God. For the Christian death is not seen as ultimate extinction or entry into oblivion. Thus the possibility for continued relationship with the deceased exists. At the

173

same time, resurrection is founded on the fact that death has occurred and has broken relationships. The Christian meaning that death and resurrection involve *both* continuity and discontinuity should be conveyed by the funeral. The passages most often cited in funeral rituals are from I Corinthians 15. This classic treatment of resurrection is not easy to understand. The concepts employed are involved and often obscure due to translation into language which, as we have seen in our earlier discussion of flesh, body, and spirit, is not fully adequate for the thought forms of earlier centuries. Understanding comes only after careful reflection. This theme of relationship with the deceased requires thoughtful interpretation in order to avoid two extremes which are not helpful to the mourning process. On one hand, the understanding of possible continued relationship must not imply that no radical change has taken place and that death is more or less illusory. On the other, acknowledgment of death's discontinuity should not imply that it cannot be overcome even by God.

Other meanings conveyed in the customarily used scriptural passages speak to the need of mourners to reflect on the meaning of their own lives and to cope with the fact of their own mortality. There are abundant passages, particularly from the Old Testament, in most funeral rituals which have as their theme the vanity or frailty of life. "Let me know how fleeting my life is" (Ps. 39:4). "Thou dost sweep men away; they are like a dream, like grass which is renewed in the morning: in the morning it flourishes and is renewed; in the evening it fades and withers" (Ps. 90:5-6).

At the same time there are references which convey the Christian understanding that in spite of the brevity of life it is lived in God's care. "The Lord will keep you from all evil; he will keep your life. The Lord will keep your going out and your coming in from this time forth and for evermore" (Ps. 121:7-8). "Thanks be to God, who gives us the victory through our Lord Jesus Christ" (I Cor. 15:57). The sense of this theme is that man can find meaning in life, though he is thoroughly mortal. Even the prospect of dying does not destroy this meaning while man lives, because it is possible for man to face death with a certain confidence and hope.

A new design for the Christian funeral will see in the scriptural passages used in the funeral a way of conveying such Christian meaning relevantly to the situation of death and bereavement. Some consideration should be given to the mourners' capacity for reception of the meanings in their particular situation. These meanings have to be geared not only to the more or less universal needs of bereaved persons but also to the particular needs of the mourners in each given situation. Care must be exercised by the pastor in selection of those passages which will be most meaningful to the particular mourners to whom he ministers. In addition, opportunity should be provided for the interpretation of those meanings that may be helpful but somewhat obscure to the mourners.

It is for this reason that a new design for the Christian funeral points to the need for reinstatement of the sermon as a part of the form of the funeral. Particularly when we seek to adapt the form of the funeral to the function of conveying meaning do we see the need and value of a funeral message. Here the pastor can respond to the need for application of meaning to the particulars of each situation. Here he has opportunity to interpret and reinterpret meanings that may tend to be obscured by the more commonly followed forms. It is not necessary to assume that a full theological understanding will be achieved at this point. But the resources of meaning need to be made available in such a way that understanding will deepen as the traumatic effects of bereavement diminish. The funeral sermon offers the possibility of presenting these meanings in a particularly relevant form because it is prepared and preached in the context of the pastor's best understanding of the needs of the mourners. It affords him the chance to convey the depth of his comprehension of their situation, their feelings, and their quest for some significance in their crisis.

The prayers which constitute a part of the form of the funeral also share in fulfilling this function of conveying Christian meaning. Here we are not so much concerned with the specific wording of the prayers as with the way in which the funeral prayers represent aspects of the Christian's relationship with God. We have in mind three fundamental aspects of that relationship: confession, gratitude, and dedication. All of these are carriers of Christian meaning.

Prayers of confession bear those meanings which have to do with the nature of life and man's reflection upon his own life. Confronted with an event that has shaken life out of its routine course, the Christian mourner is moved to make an assessment of his own life. This evaluation of man's work and his loyalties is made prayerfully, conveying the meaning that the judgment is not based on any personal standards but on God's criteria. The context of God's mercy in which Christian repentance is always undertaken provides meaning which helps man cope with his own mortality even when being very honest about his own inadequacies. If one can approach the crisis of the death of another in the framework of God's continuing care, one also finds courage to examine himself.

Prayers of gratitude are also meaningful forms in the funeral. There is gratitude for the care of God which death cannot end ultimately and the hope which it enables. There may be thankfulness for the life which has ended and the benefits that have been known through it. In many instances relationship with the deceased may be remembered in gratitude.

The prayers of intercession which comprise a major portion of many funeral rituals carry a number of meanings. Among them are the insufficiency of man to meet his deepest needs alone, the dependence which one has on God, and the trustworthiness of God to help him. In a sense this is one of the

176

ways in which Christian meaning is brought to bear on the immensity and the profundity of man's need in the face of death. Intercessory prayer is also a part of the community participation of the funeral. Although the entire group shares in the loss of the deceased, it is readily recognized that this loss is more acute for some than for others. In prayer, members of the group in their common worship intercede on behalf of those whose lives have been most deeply affected.

Other prayers are ways in which the bereaved, having faced their own mortality and assessed their living, dedicate themselves to the living out of the meanings which the Christian funeral conveys. In this way there is a strong affirmation of the purposefulness and meaningfulness of life even when confronting death. If form is to follow function, this must be a significant part of the rationale of the funeral prayers. There is no place for easy, cheap comfort that seeks to provide reassurance without accepting the pain and that substitutes pious aphorisms for a realistic understanding of death and bereavement.

What has been said here about such components of the funeral as Scripture, sermon, and prayers is equally applicable to all the accompanying funeral practices. To illustrate: I have earlier sought to demonstrate how the view of man as a totality is a part of the meaning of the Christian understanding of life and death. This meaning of totality needs to be manifested in all the funeral. It has an effect on the proper balance for regarding the physical body of the deceased. This Christian meaning will prevent funeral customs from going to extremes in the direction of either materialism or spiritualism. The meaning of totality will not be conveyed if the body becomes the entire focus of the funeral or if the appearance or preservation of the body is the major goal of the funeral. By the same token, this meaning will not be adequately presented if the funeral completely ignores or avoids any attention given to the body. In this fashion, all funeral practices need to be evaluated according to the meanings which the funeral is to present. The meanings of the Christian view of life and death, of the relationship with the deceased, and of the need for coping with awareness of one's own mortality must be regarded as determinative influences on the form of the funeral.

REINFORCING REALITY

A third major function of the funeral is the reinforcement of the reality of death. The funeral is a means for enabling the individual to acknowledge his loss. Not only does it provide a way of dramatizing the loss and what it means to the individual, it also, as we have said, affords a supportive relational framework in which the weight of reality can be tolerated and the painful process of reorientation begun.

To follow this function it is necessary that the form of the funeral have a note of authenticity. It would probably be naïve to insist that everything has to appear exactly as it really is. Life just is not lived that way. However, it is possible to strive to reduce to a minimum the disguises of reality and to work toward the full recognition that disguises are involved. It would probably be expecting too much to propose the removal of all the accouterments of the funeral that are provided to make it more aesthetically pleasing: the cosmetics applied to make the corpse more presentable, the simple flowers which relieve the starkness of the situation, the artificial grass covering the excavated grave. Such things do damage when they are taken seriously, when they complete the illusion of unreality, when they participate in the grand disguise of death as life. If that is their purpose, they should be resisted.

The new design for the Christian funeral should not lend itself to any *serious* attempt to disguise reality. In a sense what is required here is what the Danish philosopher-theologian Kierkegaard called humor. (This is no effort here to be facetious—to seek to make a sad occasion humorous.) Humor, in Kierkegaard's sense, is the capacity to see inadequacies and imperfections in something and still to maintain the capacity to hold it in high regard. Applied to reality in the funeral this would mean that one could see the imperfections manifested by the efforts to improve appearances without being drawn into the trap of losing regard for reality and falling victim to illusion. Whatever efforts are made to improve appearances should be restricted to the peripheral—removing the pallor of the corpse or covering a pile of dirt. But these minor embellishments must *never* be used to hide the fact that death has occurred, that relationships have been severed, that a new focus for life must be found by the bereaved.

The new design for the Christian funeral must face death honestly. There must be no attempt to run from it nor to avoid it. Euphemisms need not be employed. There should be no effort to disguise the fact that we are dealing with the *dead* body of a loved one, with an open grave. The language of the funeral service and the intent of funeral practices need to be evaluated carefully to see whether they are merely minor aesthetic touches or major attempts to deny the reality of death. This judgment cannot be made apart from all the Christian meanings discussed above.

Probably the central point in this whole issue is the corpse, the body of the deceased. It often has been regarded as a means for creating the illusion of life instead of facing the reality of death. It has been regarded as asleep rather than dead; it has been treated to give the illusion of imperishability; it has been the object of feelings which will not admit that death has changed relationships. So there have been proposals, many of them thoughtful, that getting rid of the body from the funeral entirely would avoid these illusions.

But it is also possible to argue that surrounded by the proper meanings, the presence of the dead body can be a significant means for reinforcing the reality of death and loss. If we have regard for the wholeness of man, his body, now dead, cannot be discarded unthinkingly. It provides a tangibility to the situation that counteracts possible attempts to make it all seem like a bad dream. It offers a focus through which the mourners help each other to validate reality. The presence of a physical object which all of them see is a means of consensually validating the real situation.

Thus a new design for the Christian funeral will have a place for the body of the deceased, not as a prop for illusions of somnolent life but as a tangible focus for apprehending the fact that death has truly taken place.

SANCTIONING AUTHENTIC FEELINGS

Another function of the Christian funeral is to make it possible for the bereaved to acknowledge and express their feelings. The mourner needs to be freed to give release to the great variety of feelings which may be welling up in him. Some of these feelings may be verbalized or acted out in the funeral. This is not to say that the feelings will all emerge fully at the exact time of the funeral. But it is one of the functions of the funeral to provide a pattern of freedom and acceptance which will permit the emergence and assimilation of the feelings as the mourning process goes on.

The form of the Christian funeral must be shaped so that it provides openness rather than restriction. The funeral may stir emotions, but this is not its primary function. In fact, even as a lesser objective it must be questioned, for the manipulative stimulation of emotions is hardly helpful. Rather, one can see the funeral as a means of creating a climate of acceptance within which the feelings that a person already has can be recognized and expressed. In the Christian funeral, the community of faith sanctions the emergence of the mourner's feelings. Even though in some instances his feelings may be too strong or too negative to come to the public view at the time of the funeral, no impediment is put in the way of their later expression in private. Hostility or guilt may not be openly brought out in the funeral, but nothing will be said or done there that will prevent their being dealt with in personal encounter at another time.

The content of the funeral ritual should carry out this function. The scriptural selections and prayers should convey understanding and acceptance of the feelings of the mourners, the sorrow which accompanies death, the pain of separation. Care should be taken not to seek to dictate what feelings the mourners should be having. It should not be implied that the Christian needs to exhibit joy or resignation or courage if this is not what he is feeling. The church must indicate, if only by implication, that it is willing to accept bitterness or guilt or despair as well.

Too often in the past one of the important criteria for judging elements of the funeral was: Will it cause an expression of feelings? On this basis proposals have been made to render the funeral coldly impersonal because references to the deceased brought tears to the eyes of the mourners. Others have suggested that the body of the deceased be eliminated from the funeral because it becomes a focus for the feelings of the bereaved. Still others have urged that funerals be as brief as possible, to the point of being perfunctory, to minimize the emotional involvement of the mourners.

The new design for the Christian funeral will rather adopt as a criterion: Will the funeral permit and even encourage the mourners to accept their feelings toward their situation, toward the deceased, and toward themselves? There are several ways in which the form of the funeral can reflect that criterion. The public form of the Christian funeral can bear witness to the fact that the community of faith is fully willing to understand and accept the feelings of the mourners. The order of the burial service of the Mar Thoma Church of South India contains the statement: "It is meet and right for everyone to be sorry for one's own departed: since death is real parting from life here, it is just and proper to weep." An effort to screen a bereaved family from the community, to privatize the funeral, carries the implication that this community is unable or unwilling to accept and share in the expression of the mourner's feelings.

The Christian faith will be understood as an affirmation that God's sustaining care provides the strength to face the painful feelings of bereavement and that the faith does not demand inhibition or elimination of all feelings. The theme of acceptance which permeates the Christian concept of grace is at the very heart of all worship and should be thoroughly evident in the funeral.

AFFIRMING FINALITY

Yet another function of the Christian funeral is to mark a fitting conclusion to the life of the one who has died. It may be thought of as a ritual of separation. It is also a ritual of transition, a benediction upon the deceased, as in Christian confidence he is commended into the hands of God. Yet there is a sense in which the radical discontinuity of death from life makes itself felt in sensing the ending of relationship as it has been known.

Death is of such significance, or for some is such a threat, that some means of marking its occurrence has been established in virtually every human society. A number of goals are involved in such an effort. It is a way of affirming the effect which the death of an individual has upon the relationships which that person has sustained with others. This is a dual affirmation in the funeral. On one hand, there is the expression of a confident hope that through resurrection a continuity of identity will make new relationship possible. On the other hand, there is a striking awareness that death has ended relationship as it has been known. One of the functions of the funeral is to dramatize this finality.

There are several forms in which the funeral can accomplish this purpose. The realistic way in which the funeral causes one to face death is involved. Realism is supported by the presence of the body of the deceased. It is sustained by a disavowal of the goals of long-term perservation. It is supported by the practice at the conclusion of the funeral of disposing of the body of the deceased, whether by burial or cremation.

The meanings contained in the Christian ritual also can fulfill this function. Death should be portrayed in terms of *both* the continuity and discontinuity which it involves. To overbalance either of these poles renders the funeral less effective in carrying out this function. If the funeral rests solely on the theme of existence after death, the finality of death from the human perspective may be regarded as illusory. If, by misinterpreting the hope for resurrection as the avoidance of death, total emphasis is laid on the inability of death to touch the Christian, finality will be empty of meaning.

The new design for the Christian funeral will strive to maintain the paradox of continuity and discontinuity in such a way that death is not circumvented but is properly seen as endured and overcome. Continuity rests upon the hope for new life given by God. Discontinuity is seen in the realistic acceptance of the fact that death brings life to an end.

The function of fittingly marking the conclusion of life also involves ways in which honor and respect can be shown for the one who has died. This does not mean an extravagant display of esteem by planning a lavish funeral or expensive memorials. This is no effort to deify the dead. Rather it is a recognition that death is an intensely personal thing. If we do not isolate death from life, we can see that a man's death is as distinctly individual and personal as his life. To pay no attention to his demise is a depersonalizing measure just as much as it is to pay no attention to his living. Sophocles in his *Antigone* bore ancient witness to this fact. In a real way, marking the death of a person is a means of testifying to the worthwhileness of his living.

The Christian funeral can accomplish this purpose because man is viewed as he is seen by God. The form in which this is carried out is not eulogy or any other effort to describe the individual's worth in glowing, or even exaggerated, terms. Such eulogization is unnecessary if God's relationship to man is the criterion of value. This understanding is founded upon a devastatingly candid appraisal of a man's strength and weakness. It finds a worth in man that is not produced by his accomplishments nor destroyed by his failures. Man's value is grounded in God's concern for him and involvement in his existence. It is this worth that is affirmed by the Christian funeral which sees man, living or dead, in relationship with God.

This context of relationship and the hope for God's gift of new life structure the conclusion of the funeral as committal. The deceased is committed to God in the confidence inspired by awareness of the relationship with God.

Too often the funeral has been used to minimize finality or to emphasize beginnings without endings. Death has been portrayed in such a way that it involves no truly major change. There has been confusion of the proximate result of death with its ultimate result according to the Christian hope. Naïve misinterpretation or willful misunderstanding can cause man to minimize death because of a total focus upon the hope for new life. The dimensions of proximity and ultimacy must always be applied, even in interpreting such a text as "Whoever lives and believes in me shall never die" (John 11:26). Still more is this careful delineation made necessary by some of the nonliturgical resources, prose and poetry, which emphasize the "there is no death" theme.

A new design for the Christian funeral will take very seriously the way in which the funeral actually symbolizes the ending of a life that has been intensely personal and of real worth because of its relationship with the Source of life. Commitment to God's care is the most suitable form to carry this meaning because at the same time it affirms that death has come to sever the ties with life as it has been known and

184

that death is not ultimate extinction. The form of the funeral must contain a sense of benediction to mark the conclusion of a life within the context of a relationship that modifies the ultimacy of that finality. While for man death is final, for God death is not final.

NEW DESIGN AND FUNERAL CUSTOMS

While we are still discussing the design of the religious funeral, there are several elements of funeral custom which need some comment. We have already examined ways in which the presence of the body may be helpful in fulfilling the function of the funeral. The question often arises whether the coffin should be open or closed during the service. Many pastors insist that it should be closed, feeling that the body in view during the funeral detracts from the comfort that is given and diminishes the spiritual emphasis. Many funeral directors urge that the casket remain open, sometimes perhaps feeling that this justifies the extensive preparation of the body. In a sense, none of these reasons are good.

A fairly strong case can be made for closing the coffin before the funeral service, although this does not need to be regarded as an absolute necessity. It would seem that the most valid reason for closing the casket is that the body is still present, although not visible, as a focus in the experience of the mourners, but there is symbolically the beginning of the separation and the sense of the finality of changed relationship. A reasonable design would be then for the body to be viewed by the mourners at times prior to the funeral. The body would be present, but the casket would be closed for the funeral itself and probably would not be reopened after the funeral.

Time is another important consideration which needs to be taken into account in proposals for a new design for the funeral. We have sought to point out earlier the importance of group participation in the funeral in order to fulfill a num-

185

ber of its vital functions. We have also indicated that a limited survey reports that in a number of areas of the nation the funeral is attended by a much smaller number of people than participate in the viewing at the mortuary on the day prior to the funeral. Many pastors report that fewer people attend funerals than did some years ago. It has often been suggested that this pattern is caused largely by the time persons have available. In our present economic and social structure, people find it difficult to take time from their work to attend a funeral for other than a very close relative. In former days many more people were self-employed or were sufficiently related to their employer to arrange for time off to attend a funeral. In addition to this, we must remember that many more women are now employed than were formerly, removing them from the ranks of those whose schedule permits funeral attendance.

The problem appears quite simply to be that the customary afternoon or morning hour for the funeral severely limits community participation beyond the immediate family in most urban oriented sections. The only way in which friends and more distant relatives can participate in the social ritual is by attending the evening visitation. The fact that these events are commonly well attended would seem to indicate that there is still a desire to be a part of the funerary observances even though economic and social circumstances seem to require a new form of participation.

We shall explore in greater detail in the next chapter what we regard to be the advantages of the funeral over the viewing as a part of the mourning process. Our question here is: How can it be made more convenient for persons beyond the immediate family to take part in the funeral?

The most obvious answer is to adjust the commonly followed time schedule of the funeral. There is nothing sacrosanct about an early afternoon hour. A number of possibilities suggest themselves, depending largely upon the situation of the community in which the funeral takes place. When can the community (family and congregation) gather? In many communities an early evening hour may be more feasible. The major problem here would be the committal service. It would be highly impractical to go to a cemetery at night for burial. It would be equally undesirable to conclude the funeral completely for the family and have the body removed for burial at a later time by the staff of the funeral director. This would remove the family from one of the forms which most adequately fulfills the function of symbolizing finality. It would be more helpful to consider the possibility of the immediate family, together with the pastor and funeral director, taking the body to the cemetery for committal on the following morning. Where cremation is used, as will unquestionably be more and more the case in urban areas, there will be no problem, for the committal at the crematory can take place in the evening as well as during the day.

It may be that socio-economic changes in the not too distant future, involving a shortening of the work week for many employees, will produce a daily schedule that would be more adaptable to convenient attendance. If a shortening of the working day is the result, late afternoon funerals may be the answer. If a longer weekend is forthcoming, daytime funerals might be in order on work-free days.

Individual solutions will suggest themselves for each community and congregation. To explore all the possibilities is hardly our purpose. The point we would make with emphasis is that attendance at the funeral is an important factor in fulfilling the functions of the funeral. The functions press us to make the form of the service, particularly with regard to time, more flexible in order to assure the broadest possible participation. Churches might well give some attention to the development of their own proposed solutions for this problem.

Another part of the design of the Christian funeral involves the place in which it is held. Here again there is no absolute requirement, but it is possible to present the case for a strong and logical preference. The most appropriate place for the Christian funeral is in the church. This is not because God is localized or worship is more valid in one place than another. Nor is it a matter of competition between the sacred and the secular. Nor is it an effort to get the funeral into territory where the practices of the church will overrule those of the funeral director. These are all specious reasons.

It is far more reasonable to argue that the church is the tangible site of the corporate life of the community which is actively participating in a meaningful way in the funeral service. The community can certainly gather elsewhere, but there is a given place where its existence comes into focus most clearly. Symbolically, the gathering of the congregation to share its mutual sorrow and to affirm its common hope is an expression of solidarity which is of real help to the mourners.

The church funeral is also a means for connecting, rather than separating, life and death. In the church building there are regular services of worship, there are baptisms and marriages. To hold the funeral in a place that is related to many phases of life deepens these associations with all of life. This is not an effort to dilute death, to put it into "happy" or "normal" surroundings. That would be an escapist technique. Rather, this becomes a means by which life and death are brought into deeper association, and death is truly seen as a meaningful part of a meaningful life.

Finally, regarding the Christian funeral, as a religious service it is logical and fitting that it be guided by the pastor. The pastor is an interpreter of the heritage of the church, and one of his functions is to seek to make the ministering of the church to human need as relevant, meaningful, and helpful as possible. Thus, the pastor in guiding the funeral has the responsibility to employ the broadest and best criteria. Too often pastors have not fully exercised this responsibility. They have been too rigid to be able to adapt form to function. Funerals have often been perfunctory or have become sterile formalities. Pastors have too often been limited in their understanding of human needs, failing to be relevant. Some sought only to evangelize, or to dispense comfort without any indication of real awareness of need. The pastor must give serious study to the functions of the funeral and must engage in a constant effort to enable the forms of the funeral to fulfill those functions.

The religious funeral has the possibility of relating all needs of the bereaved to the resources found in relationship with God and with the community of faith. A constant effort is required to adapt its forms to the fulfillment of its functions.

The Humanistic Funeral

In all candor, we must acknowledge that the religious elements of the funeral are not meaningful to all. If the funeral is seen only as a religious service, it either denies to the non-religious person some of the nonreligious values because he cannot participate in its meanings, or it compels him to participate hypocritically and therefore without meaning. While I might not personally agree with the presuppositions of the nonreligious person or the humanist, it is a legitimate concern for me that the funeral should be a helpful part of the mourning process when he is bereaved. There are still a number of valuable functions which the funeral can fulfill for the humanist.

Perhaps the task of exploring the function and forms of the humanistic funeral should be left to someone of that persuasion rather than for a Christian minister to make the effort. Yet, this so often results only in a proposal from the nonreligious person that the funeral should be discarded altogether. It is hoped that this study has effectively presented

189

a picture of both the religious and the nonreligious values of the funeral. These values are by no means identical, yet each has its own kind of validity. A humanistic funeral is possible and can be helpful.

Very little consideration has been given to the nontheistic funeral. Practically no exploration has been made of its distinctive functions. The only major existing resource is Lamont's booklet [1] which presents a service of the order that we are discussing. While it is helpful and there is much to commend it, this humanist service has several flaws which need to be pointed out. Occasionally it lapses into a dualism that is somewhat inconsistent with its humanistic principles. In other instances it becomes a virtual paraphrase of the Christian service, citing Plato instead of the Bible but seeking to convey identical meaning. In spite of these minor difficulties, it does provide one resource for describing a humanistic funeral. It sees value in the functions of the funeral and reflects a good understanding of many needs of the mourners.

The particular presuppositions which seem to be involved in varying combinations for those who desire the humanistic funeral are these: Man's existence is totally and ultimately limited to the space and time relationships we call life. Death brings these relationships to an end and marks the termination of personal identity. There is, however, the possibility of some kind of social or biological immortality, the living on of the person's influence through his descendants or his contributions to society. Secondly, it is assumed that the present life contains all of the possibilities and resources that a man possesses. There is a self-sufficiency in man's existence. Thirdly, relationship is seen in a single dimension, person to person, with no reference to a transcendent dimension—man with God.

We would maintain that these presuppositions most as-

---

[1] Corliss Lamont, A Humanist Funeral Service.

suredly modify the funeral as seen from a Christian perspective, but they do not destroy all the values of the funeral as they have been described in the previous section. Of course the functions of these two kinds of funerals are not identical, but there are distinct values to be derived through humanistic or nonreligious functions of the funeral.

SUPPORTIVE RELATIONSHIPS

The first function of the funeral has to do with the supportive framework of relationship which is to be provided for the mourners. The form through which the humanistic funeral fulfills this purpose is the gathering of family and friends to share in a time of sorrow. The identity of this group is constituted almost solely by some form of relationship with the deceased through kinship or association. The group in many instances may have no other identity, no other point in common.

The mutual relationship and shared loss draw this group together for a ceremony marking the end of a life and their common needs for support. As one of the group has died, the survivors lean upon one another for strength to assimilate their loss. In their sympathy they find support. This function of the group is limited to the hour of the ceremony because of the absence of a continuing group identity. Individuals may continue their supportive aid to the mourners, but they do so solely on the basis of personal relationships. This aid is directed by the desires of the individual rather than by an institutional structure which channels the activity of the group.

The design for the humanistic funeral will seek to draw together such a group. It must provide some form which will enable individual members of the group to participate. The *ad hoc* nature of the group makes this more difficult because the absence of a common heritage as a group means that there are no readily available stable forms for group participation. There are no hymns, no common affirmations of faith,

191

no traditional prayers. There is no reason, however, why a humanistic funeral ceremony should not contain brief sections that can be read in unison by those in attendance. If the humanistic funeral is to become a reality, some forms will have to be forthcoming for public use. These should provide means for some participation in the ritual by all those in attendance, testifying to the mutuality of their support and stirring individuals in the group to continue their support of the mourners even after the group disbands.

MEANINGS

The second function of the funeral is to convey relevant meanings of life and death. The meanings that are involved grow out of the presuppositions of the humanistic philosophy. One of the most important of these is that life and death must be seen as fully related because seeing death should cause one to reflect on the values and meanings of life. The goal of humanism is the deepening and improvement of man's living. Confrontation of death is one of the means to this end. In the humanistic funeral it is possible to bring life and death into conjunction by seeing them both as parts of the natural process. Man lives as a part of nature and as a participant in the natural order he dies. Death is regarded as the perfectly natural and inevitable outcome of his living.

The major emphasis which this position would affirm is that the brevity of life and the inevitability of its ending are accented in bereavement and that man is convinced of the need to live his short life to the fullest. Meaningful relationship between death and life is intended to enable man to make the maximum investment in his living.

Another area to which meanings are applied is the way in which death changes relationship to the deceased. There is no question that death severs this relationship. Death is regarded as the absolute ending of existence so there is no doubt that further actual relationship is impossible. The only possibilities are a relationship in memory and a kind of immortality in the contributions one's life has made to posterity. One may recall relationship with the dead in the past, but there is no regard for any possibility of relationship in time to come.

Still other meanings in the funeral must help the mourner to cope with awareness of his own death. Here the humanistic funeral finds its resources for this confrontation in the support of the group and in recognition that one is caught up in the natural processes of living and dying. Death cannot be overcome, but by the collective action of the group it is made less forbidding. Likewise, there is no need to fear death because it is part of the natural order of things. Each individual confronts death in the company of all other living things. Some strength is found in acknowledging death to be universal and impersonal. Since death can be accepted in these ways, the individual is to devote his energy to living the fullest possible life in the time that is his.

The form by which these meanings are communicated is a series of affirmations based on the reflections of a member of the group or on the writings of philosophers and poets collected in funeral resource books or services such as that prepared by Lamont. Others might find less sophisticated sources more meaningful. Since such a ceremony requires no external authority, these meanings could be appropriately selected or phrased by the individual conducting the funeral. It should be stressed, however, that such formulations need to be developed with sensitive awareness of the functions that the funeral is seeking to fulfill.

A design for the humanistic funeral will have to make provision for conveying these central meanings: death is a part of life and must be confronted to help man face life purposefully; death ends all relationship with the deceased except a relationship of memory based on his contributions to life; the mourner is enabled to cope with reflection upon his own death by acknowledgment that death is natural, universal, and impersonal.

One of the ceremonial acts of the humanistic funeral which could also help to fulfill this function is the act of committal of the body to nature. Whether this be burial or cremation, there is opportunity here to indicate the way in which man is regarded as a part of nature. The act becomes an important testimonial to the way in which individual life is regarded as rejoining the natural elements.

REINFORCING REALITY

A third function of the funeral is the reinforcement of reality. The humanistic funeral does not need to disguise death. Since death is seen as a part of the natural process, there should be no need to sentimentalize it nor to veil it with illusion. The form of the humanistic funeral must be a reminder that death is a part of the lot of every man. Every living thing comes to the end of its life. The regularity and the inexorability of the processes of nature strengthen the desire to affirm natural death as real. The humanistic funeral should contain assertions of this reality.

The body of the deceased also has a place in the humanistic funeral. It is understood as a physical object—real, palpable. It is acknowledged as a dead body. Since there is no place in the monistic presuppositions of the humanist stance for any dimension other than physical, the point should be very clear. Death, as manifested by the corpse, has brought an end to vitality and activity. The final committal, whatever its form, provides further validation of this reality.

SANCTIONING AUTHENTIC FEELINGS

The fourth function of the funeral is to provide an openness to the awareness of and expression of the feelings of the mourners. The group which gathers for the humanistic funeral is drawn by mutual association with the deceased and by a common loss. It is to be hoped that the group is thus in a position to understand and accept the feelings of those who are most deeply affected by the loss.

Since the group's identity is only temporary, its sanction of the feelings of the mourners may not have the carry-over quality of the acceptance of a more permanent group. But still it is a vital part of the funeral that in both word and attitude the rights of the mourners to express what they really are feeling are affirmed.

The form of the funeral may contain references to the naturalness of deep emotions when death has come near. Separation from the deceased, which is an obvious consequence of the humanistic presuppositions, stirs feelings which are understandable and acceptable. The fact that these feelings remain until they have been thoroughly ventilated can also be indicated. The one who conducts the funeral should be aware of the possibility of negative feelings in some instances. While these probably are not identified openly, the funeral is to imply the acceptance of all feelings of the mourners. Since death is seen as natural, it is possible also to see the response of the living to death as natural.

AFFIRMING FINALITY

The fifth function of the funeral is to mark fittingly the conclusion of a life. The form of the humanistic funeral can follow this function in a number of ways. There is here an opportunity to honor and commemorate the contributions which have been made by the life of the deceased. The belief in social and biological immortality means that this contribution lives on in the mourners themselves. This does not necessarily require glowing eulogy. The acknowledgment that a contribution has been made and received may be quite sufficient.

The fittingness of the conclusion also means that a strong personal element should be present in the humanistic funeral.

Even though death is emphasized as natural and universal, there is a distinctly personal quality involved as well. There is a uniqueness in each man's dying, just as there is in his living. An individual life has come to its close. It should be clear that the gathered group at the funeral is responding to its association with a person, an association which is now terminated.

Finality is recognized in the form of the funeral. Life has ended; relationships have been severed. The only bond now with the deceased is the bond of memory. It is vital that memories are acknowledged to be just that. They are not means for recreating the past or restoring relationship. Death has taken place and the past is irretrievable.

The form of the humanistic funeral is to represent death as final. It affirms that while memory is possible, one who has died exists only in the past. One can give honor to the deceased without trying to create the illusion of present existence. The committal represents this finality as the body, acknowledged as a part of nature, is returned to the natural elements.

In general, the form of the humanistic funeral will seek to fulfill these functions. How such a form can develop is yet to be seen. This is a difficult problem for several reasons. There is no permanence for the assembled group, so there is no stable identity out of which a ceremony can grow. There are, at least at present, few professional leaders who would have responsibility for the formulation and perpetuation of a ceremony, such as the clergy does in the church. In all probability a ritual such as Lamont's service can become the basis of popular practice. Particular communities would then tend to make such modifications as they deem necessary. It is also likely that other individuals of this persuasion would develop and publish ceremonies for use. Whatever their source, it is to be hoped that such rituals will reflect a full and accurate understanding of the functions of the funeral.

196

A related question is: Who shall conduct the humanistic funeral? It might be possible for a minister of the church to lead such a ceremony out of concern for the needs of individuals who have no relationship with the church. The artificiality in which he now finds himself in seeking to minister through a Christian ceremony which lacks meaning for the mourners is relieved. He would be using a humanistic service for those whose orientation is humanistic. In order to maintain his own integrity, he would certainly need an opportunity to explain his position; to point out that he acts as a Christian individual concerned that mourners receive the comfort and strength that is possible for them in their own framework of meanings, rather than as a pastor conducting one of the rites of the church. This sort of arrangement would probably be the exception to the rule.

It would seem far more logical that the funeral director or a member of his staff conduct the humanistic funeral. It may well be that a person or persons in a given community would emerge as the leaders of such funerals. There is already something of a parallel in those individuals who conduct various fraternal rituals in connection with deaths. Whoever they may be, hopefully such individuals would seek to deepen their understanding of bereavement and the ways in which mourners are helped. If these proposals for a humanistic funeral are taken seriously and if such would become a custom, suitable resources to assist these leaders in their responsibility would be forthcoming.

The function of the funeral has a bearing on the place in which the humanistic funeral is held. The home of the deceased would be the logical location as a means for bringing life and death into conjunction. It would be highly appropriate to memorialize the ending of a life in a place which was the familiar setting for the living of that life. However, realistically it must be recognized that in many communities the home of the deceased would not be a practical place for

197

the funeral because of limitations of space and accessibility. A public auditorium or place of assembly, preferably one associated with events of the living, might be a more reasonable substitute.

From the standpoint of equipment, facilities, and availability, it is quite likely that the most feasible place for the humanistic funeral is the funeral home, even though it has, as we have indicated earlier, the one disadvantage of being singularly associated with death. This concern is not a matter of simple aesthetics nor of superstitious taboos. It represents the fact that the funeral fulfills its functions more adequately if every means is used to see death as a part of life rather than as an intrusion.

A question remains: Is the religious (or the humanistic) orientation of the deceased or of the major mourners determinative of the funeral practice which should be followed, assuming that there is a difference of orientation present? What should be the nature of the funeral of a humanist whose mourners are Christian or of a Christian whose mourners are humanists? On the basis of the functions we have described in detail, it would seem that the orientation of the major mourners would be the indicator of whether the funeral should be religious or humanistic. Since most of the functions focus on the needs of the bereaved, such a decision seems logical.

But we must also remember that the funeral is not totally divorced from nor indifferent to the life which has ended. It would not seem altogether inappropriate to mark the conclusion of a Christian life, for example, with a Christian funeral, even though the major mourners are humanists. Here flexibility is essential. In such situations the pastor needs to attempt to relate Christian meanings to the life that has ended, while at the same time seeking to minister to the needs of the humanistic mourners within the scope of their receptive capabilities. Such a funeral is in one sense a testimony of the faith of the deceased, but that witness is sterile unless

198

there is concern for the capacity of the mourners to receive it. Again it becomes apparent how necessary a sensitivity to the needs of the mourners is for the proper conduct of the funeral.

The proposal of two types of funerals reflects something of the thought of Bossard [2] in his description of transformations being made in family rituals. He sees ritual changing from predominance of the religious to predominance of the secular. Rituals in the present time tend to involve smaller groups than they once did. The group which is engaged in the ritual tends to be mobile rather than stable. The nature of the group reflects a shift from a family surrounded by a neighborhood to a group which is isolated within the urban environment.

We have noted some similar changes in the funeral. We are not suggesting that this is an inevitable development nor that it is even desirable. It is, however, a fairly accurate appraisal of the changes which are taking place in many situations of bereavement.

The important thing for us to note is that Bossard is suggesting that changes are taking place in the structure of family rituals, but he is not proposing that rituals be discontinued. Ceremony does serve a useful function. It transmits meanings, it provides a matrix in which existing feelings can be channeled, it meets human need. Since it is an experience of value, ritual needs to be given constant evaluation to make possible its maximum utilization. It is for this reason that we suggest the humanistic funeral, not as a replacement for nor competitor of the religious funeral but as a supplementary alternative.

[2] James Bossard and Eleanor Boll, *Ritual in Family Living* (Philadelphia: University of Pennsylvania Press, 1950), pp. 21-26.

9

Responding to Other
Emerging Patterns

There are a number of developments in funeral practice in our day to which our position must respond. The new designs for the funeral which are being suggested in this study have something to say in evaluating such trends as the custom of viewings held at the funeral home, the disposition of the body by cremation or bequest, the memorial service held in lieu of the funeral, and the privatization of the funeral.

Viewings and Funerals

In the past it was the custom in many communities to have the body of the deceased "laid out" in the family home where friends and relatives came to call. Sometimes this period was the occasion for rather elaborate wakes. More recently it has become the practice in most areas of the nation to hold viewings of the deceased in a funeral home prior to the funeral. These are hours when friends offer sympathy and support to the bereaved. Experience is proving that in many communities more people take part in the viewing than in the funeral.

A number of reasons can be advanced to explain this trend. We have already suggested that there is more participation in the viewing because it takes place at an hour that is more convenient for most people. It is also true that in many instances it involves considerably less expenditure of time, be-

cause the informality of the viewing is not bound to a structured schedule. Persons come and go at will.

Another possible reason for the growing participation in
the viewing may well be the decline in group activity in so
much of our social process. The viewing is primarily a series
of personal visits rather than a group congregating. The activity is individual rather than corporate. This is true of much
of contemporary living where society lacks strong formal group
identity. Even the church is seen by some as having outgrown
the parochial form, needing to develop a life apart from any
structured group. The associations of life are so diverse that
rarely would a single group encompass all those who want
to participate in some way in the activities surrounding the
death of a given person. Consequently, the activity that is
individualistic rather than corporate is preferred.

Still another reason for attendance at the viewing is for
some the absence of ceremony. The viewing is a quasi-social
event, often called the "visitation." There is nothing wrong
with this per se. There are, from community to community,
certain matters of protocol which are observed, but normally
the viewing is not accompanied by ceremony. There are a few
exceptions, such as the recitation of the rosary by Roman
Catholics or the conduct of the ritual of a fraternal order
in connection with the viewing. But for some the fact that
the viewing is not usually ceremonial may be its real appeal.
They prefer to attend the viewing because they do not find
meaning in the funeral ritual. In this sense the viewing can
be seen for some as a primordial form of the humanistic
funeral.

Yet one other reason for increased participation in the
viewing may be the desire on the part of many individuals for
a point of personal contact with the mourners that may not
be available in the funeral.

The increasing involvement in the practice of viewing may
also be the result of conformity growing out of social inertia.

Patterns established in communities tend to perpetuate themselves without necessary connection to their original causes. What we are really saying is that in some circumstances there may be no real reason why people attend the viewing rather than the funeral. It has just become the thing to do.

We would not suggest that funerals and viewings are mutually exclusive. There are certain advantages which they both offer; there are other values which each can afford. One of the major common advantages which each of these events provides is the presence of the body of the deceased as a focus for the feelings and expression of feelings of all who take part.

The distinctive advantages of the funeral rest mainly in its ceremonial aspects. The funeral has a ritual structure which, as we have seen, is a systematic communication of meanings designed to enable mourners to assimilate their experience. The value of this ritual is augmented by the participation of a group out of which the ritual, in essence, has grown. The structure of the funeral in itself is valuable because on the basis of the accrued experience of many persons who have suffered bereavement it seeks to provide for the needs of the present mourners. Without this kind of ritual structure, each bereavement would begin de novo to seek by trial and error to find relief.

The particular advantages of the viewing lie in the direct interpersonal communication with the mourners. Because of the informal nature of the event, face-to-face conversations are possible in which friends and relatives can talk with the mourners about the deceased, about their recollections of former days, about their common feelings of loss, about their desire to provide support. Many aspects of the mourning process are sanctioned and encouraged in the customs which surround viewings: learning to live with memories of the deceased; awareness of and expression of feelings toward the deceased, his death, and oneself; realization that in relationship there is healing to be found. In a very real sense the actual presence

202

of the body is an important aid at this point. Without this focus the conversation might well become totally peripheral and the socializing utterly superficial. If such were the case, the usefulness of the viewing would be drastically reduced.

We see, then, that the viewing has definite values, but we can also observe that these are not as extensive as those of the funeral. It would be limiting to claim that either could substitute completely for the other. The viewing cannot be a complete substitute for the funeral because it lacks several very important features. It has no real progression and no terminus. It is episodic and repetitive. It is a series of nearly identical visits which are practically the same at the end of the visitation period as they are at the beginning. There is no real sense in which the viewing develops a progression of meaningful insights and events, moving toward a climax such as the experience of finality which concludes the funeral. But even more than this, the viewing lacks a structure for the communication of meanings which the funeral possesses. This is not to say that the viewing is devoid of such meaning, but its highly individualistic, episodic form does not normally follow any kind of structure to enable a systematic or consistent presentation of meanings. The heterogeneous quality of the group participating in the viewing would also limit the possibility of consistent meanings being conveyed.

Both the values and the limitations of the viewing have implications for our proposals for new designs for the funeral. The funeral should offer maximum opportunity for direct interpersonal communication between the group and the major mourners. The funeral is properly understood as a group experience, involving each one who attends. The funeral ritual should give opportunity for the entire group to take part, rather than just to be observers. The whole group gives affirmation to the meanings which are being conveyed. The whole group is expressing its corporate sense of loss and its common desire to sustain those whose lives have been most deeply touched. A new design for the funeral will stress this element of communication between the participating group and the major mourners.

New designs for the funeral, stimulated by one of the frequently expressed reasons for the increasing participation in the viewing, need to take seriously into account the whole question of time and convenience. If we truly believe that the funeral is a valid portion of the whole mourning process, we need to endeavor to make wide participation as convenient and practical as possible.

The kind of communication that takes place at the viewing around the focus of the body of the deceased helps us to see that this presence is a valuable part of the design of the funeral. The body, even with some of the superficialities that accompany it, can be seen as an inescapable reminder that death has taken place and that loss must be assimilated.

In these ways the new designs for the funeral can respond constructively to the values and limitations of the viewing.

Disposition of the Body

The more or less traditional form of disposition of the dead body in America has been earth burial. In recent decades, particularly in urban areas, cremation has been gaining public favor. We need to examine these modes of disposition to determine what values they offer to new designs for the funeral.

Burial, according to a number of archaeological and anthropological studies, is probably the oldest method of disposition.[1] It has been widely employed in Western culture for many centuries.

There are several symbolic meanings which can be found in the practice of burying the dead. In one sense burial symbolizes the unity of all nature. Man, a part of nature, returns to

[1] Cf. E. O. James, *Prehistoric Religion*, pp. 97 ff.

204

the elements in burial. The familiar lines of the burial office read: "Earth to earth, ashes to ashes, dust to dust." Burial is a way in which the actual physical structure of the body breaks down again into its elemental components. Another variation of this symbolic meaning is the return to mother earth. Eliade [2] points out that in some cultures where it is customary for adults to be cremated, the bodies of children are buried in the earth in hope that having reentered the womb of mother earth they may be reborn.

The symbolism of burial also provides for a locus, a point of reference, for remembering the dead. The site of the burial can be visited as a stimulus for remembering the deceased and relationships with him. However, we need to be aware of the danger that some may recast this meaning in terms of assuming the presence of the deceased in the grave. Some morbid grief reactions are based upon efforts to sustain relationships with the deceased on the basis of frequent visits to the grave, as if one were "visiting" the person. More often, though, burial and the marking of the grave are regarded as tangible reminders that a particular person has lived and died.

The purposes of burial are fairly obvious. Although among primitive people burial was sometimes a means for seeking to control the malevolent spirit of the dead, its function is more properly regarded in a practical sense. It is a means of disposing of the body of the dead in a manner which avoids contamination, employing the earth as one of the reasonable resources at hand.

Several values can be noted in the practice of burial. The committal and burial comprise a natural terminus of the funeral. Burial represents the final act in the ritual, the symbolic conclusion of the life. To the mourners it signifies that last act which is performed for the deceased. Burial also becomes for the mourners the act through which their sepa-

[2] Mircea Eliade, *Patterns in Comparative Religion*, trans. by Rosemary Sheed (New York: Sheed and Ward, 1958) p. 250.

ration from the deceased is most dramatically demonstrated. The ending of visual contact with the body of the deceased and the obvious impossibility of further interaction because of the deterioration process support the awareness that relationship with the deceased as it has been known is no longer possible. The radical discontinuity which death brings is symbolized in burial.

There are also certain difficulties involved in the custom of burial of the dead. One of these problems is the limitation of space. European countries already have found that earth burial is not feasible because so little land is available for cemeteries. Metropolitan areas in this country are facing a similar situation. Earth burial will probably become increasingly less frequent in the future in large centers of population. Another difficulty frequently cited in relation to burial is the cost. Purchase of a grave or cemetery lot with perpetual care contract, a vault, a monument, and labor for opening the grave can account for a sizable portion of the expense of the funeral. Thus there have been proposals that less expensive means be found for disposing of the body. Finally, if coupled with intentions of long-term preservation, burial can produce in the minds of some mourners a mistaken sense of the permanent presence of the body in the grave, possibly leading to the persistence of a morbid relationship with the deceased.

An alternative form of disposition of the body is cremation. We are thinking now of cremation after the funeral, as an alternative to earth burial.

Just as we noted symbolic meanings in burial, so too are there such meanings in cremation. This process involves a reduction of the body to its basic natural elements in immediate disintegration rather than gradual decomposition. The human body is symbolized as a part of nature which in this way is changed from the form in which it has been known into its chemical components. Throughout history cremation has conveyed varying meanings. To some it symbolized the fiery purification of the individual, the release of the pure spirit. To others it was a means of destroying the body to drive its spirit into oblivion. To still others it was a way of representing man's ultimate solidarity with the whole of nature.

After the actual burning of the body, the second phase of the cremation process is the disposition of the ashes. If these ashes are scattered there is symbolic representation of the reunion with the natural world, much like the final result of burial. If the ashes are placed in a columbarium or interred, there is provided a focus for remembrance very similar to the grave. It should be noted that there is less danger that mourners will seek to perpetuate morbid relationships with the deceased because cremation involves such obvious change through immediate dissolution.

The purposes of cremation are virtually the same as those for burial. The major difference is time. Cremation brings about the dissolution of the body quickly, compressing into a few hours the process that may in burial take months or years. Cremation is in this sense a speeding of the process of nature. It has been this point that has stirred resistance to cremation in some religious groups. The Roman Catholics, because of their strong regard for natural law, find objection to the substitution of a man-made process for a natural process. Other religious objectors may base their resistance upon a literal understanding of the resurrection of the dead body, suggesting that this would be impossible for a body totally destroyed by fire. Such objections are not widespread and will probably be modified if cremation is more widely practiced.

The values to be seen in cremation are not measurably different from those found in interment. The value of manifesting finality is very much a part of cremation. This method of disposition also affords a natural terminus for the funeral. It marks the ending of a life as it has been known. The rapid dissolution of the body indicates with considerable clarity that death has occurred, that relationships have been ended, that things can never again be as they have been in the past. Immediate dissolution of the body removes the temptation to assume that long-term preservation somehow defeats the ravages of death.

Other values which can be attributed to cremation are the tangible savings that are accomplished through it. Savings of space are obvious and constitute one of the major practical values of cremation. Economic savings also make cremation attractive. However, it should be seen that the fact that cremation is now somewhat less costly than burial does not assure that this will always remain so. If cremation were to become the most commonly utilized form of disposition, there is no guarantee that costs would not increase.

There are also some difficulties which can be encountered by misunderstanding cremation. It is conceivable that the process of rapid dissolution may be misunderstood as implying a lack of significance of the body of the deceased, even a kind of tacit disparagement of it. Such an attitude might easily foster a dualistic understanding of man's nature, dissolving the dross of the physical body in order that the pure spirit might be released. Another possible difficulty is that the mourner, if cremation is not carefully thought through, may get the feeling of having deliberately destroyed something of the deceased person. In the event of unresolved guilt or hostility such an impression might easily complicate the mourning process.

Another variant of the use of cremation should be examined at this point. It is sometimes the practice to cremate the body immediately after death and to dispose of the ashes according to the wishes of the family. At a later time a memorial service is held instead of a funeral. We shall compare the funeral to the memorial service shortly, but here we inquire into the purpose of immediate cremation followed later by a memorial service.

Although there are certainly instances in which burial is

followed by a memorial service, cremation seems to be more often associated with this format. Since the major difference between cremation and burial is largely a matter of time, it would appear that the compressing of time is seen as a value by those who prefer cremation. This sense of urgency is accented in plans for disposing of the body immediately following death. Such urgency may be motivated by a desire to avoid embalming and other preparatory processes, or by a wish to remove as soon as possible all occasion for association with the body, or by a need to avoid stimulating expressions of emotion, or by the intention to affirm indifference to the body as a significant part of the person. The reason for any sense of urgency in disposing of the body becomes crucial in our consideration of this practice.

A parallel situation is found in those fairly infrequent instances where the deceased has bequeathed his body to an institution for medical research. Without going into detail on the obvious humanitarian elements in such an arrangement, we note that as far as the mourners are concerned, disposition is immediate. After research studies have been completed, the appropriate disposition of the body usually will be carried through by the institution. For the family, however, the removal of the body from their custody is the time of disposition.

My conviction is that the method of disposition, whether by interment or cremation or bequest, can be decided on purely practical grounds once the question of accepting reality is resolved. This is the crucial issue. Any form of disposition is inferior if it is a means by which the person seeks to evade the pain of mourning, or the awareness of the reality of death, or the emotional responses involved in contact with the body of the deceased. Interment is wrong if it has implied to the mourner that the deceased has been preserved ad infinitum and that a kind of physical presence in the grave makes a form of interpersonal relationship still possible. Cremation is wrong, particularly when it is done immediately following death, if it is a way in which the mourner attempts to escape contact with death, seeks to avoid reality, or tries to remove the object which causes discomfort. As a means of simple disposition of the body of the dead, there is merit in either of the methods we have described. Individual preference can be the basis for the decision once the motivations are thoroughly clarified.

This comparison of the practices of burial and cremation advances some implications for the design of the funeral. Certainly the funeral can accommodate either method. But we must assume that the method of disposition of the body is a part of the form of the funeral and thus needs to follow the functions of the funeral. But even more than this, the motivations behind the selection of a method of disposition need to be carefully weighed in the light of these functions.

The design for the funeral must do two things. It must include an act of disposition, and it must make clear the meaning of disposition. The presence of the body at the funeral is valuable as a confirmation of the reality of death. However, the value is dissipated if this presence is not surrounded by a context that resoundingly affirms the finality that death has brought. This combination of temporary presence and final disposition is an effective means for both recalling the significance of the body as a manifestation of the total person and acknowledging that relationships as they have been known are now ended.

The design for the funeral must make clear that disposition of the body is not discarding the corpse. Such a statement is not based on sentimentality or superstition. We do not discard the body as base matter, or as an empty shell, or as carrion. This body is a dimension of a person who has died. If we affirm the value of personhood, we cannot demean any aspect of the person. The body is not discarded like rubbish but is disposed of because it is dead and because death has brought to a conclusion the quality of relationship that has been sus-

210

tained with the person. This should not be understood as a warrant for expensive or elaborate burial or cremation procedures. A pine coffin is as effective as a bronze casket. Scattered ashes are as adequate as a family mausoleum. This is not the issue. The single important question is: Does the mode of disposition of the body affirm for the mourners their awareness that death has taken place, their willingness to accept the pain of mourning, and their acknowledgment that the relationships with the deceased as they have been known have come to an end?

The Memorial Service

Another of the newer customs to which we should respond is the memorial service conducted in lieu of the funeral. The practice is not completely new. It was the custom, for example, in colonial days in New England to bury the body and then go to the church for a service of worship. The practice of some in our own day is quite similar. Within a day or so following death the body is cremated or buried privately, with only the family or some members of the family in attendance. Sometimes a brief committal service is read. Then, following an interval of a few days, a memorial service is held for the family and friends. Although this custom is not as yet widely practiced, it has often been advanced, particularly by clergymen, as an ideal replacement for the funeral. In the survey reported earlier in this book 28 percent of the ministers polled wished a memorial service to be held in lieu of a funeral at the time of their own death.

We can learn a good deal about the function and the form of the memorial service by evaluating the numerous reasons which have been advanced in its favor.

The memorial service is often recommended as more spiritual than the funeral because any emphasis on the body of the deceased is absent. Since the body has already been disposed

211

of, there is no physical focus. This is regarded by advocates of the memorial service as ideal because it enables the entire experience to center on the intellectual or the spiritual level. Those who advance this argument conclude that this spiritualization of the ceremony makes it more Christian and less pagan.

A second reason offered in favor of the memorial service is that it is less emotional than the funeral. Because the body is absent, one major stimulus for the expression of the feelings of the mourners is minimized. The service is able to proceed on an intellectual rather than an emotional level. This is intended to remove some of the strain from the bereaved. The delaying of the memorial service for several days beyond the time when the funeral normally is held is also a means for making it less emotional, for it is possible to wait until the initial trauma is well past before facing the group. The mourners have more time to compose themselves and have fewer stimuli for expressions of emotion before they enter into the public dimension of the ritual.

A third argument in support of the memorial service is that it is focused more clearly on life than on death. The absence of the major reminder of death, the corpse, makes it much easier to avoid the harshness of death and to center attention on life. The desire to avoid expressions of sorrow, which consciously or unconsciously is often a motivation for the memorial service, encourages the emphasis on life as a means for escaping some of the pain of mourning.

Other reasons for the memorial service are convenience and economy. Because disposition of the body is not involved, any time of the day or evening is suitable for the memorial service. Its time can be suited to the convenience of the participants. Furthermore, it is argued that the memorial service is less costly because it does not necessarily involve the expense of embalming and preparation of the body and the services of the funeral director beyond the simple disposition of the body either by burial or cremation. Since no public viewing is held, a very inexpensive casket can be used.

When we compare the functions and forms of the Christian memorial service with that of the Christian funeral, rightly understood and conducted, some very interesting points begin to emerge. (We deal with the Christian service as illustration. Much the same could be said for its humanistic variations.)

The strong emphasis of the memorial service with its negation of the physical by removal of the body is in contrast with the emphasis on the whole man which the funeral conveys. It must be granted that the funeral has sometimes gone to the opposite extreme, overemphasizing the material. However, the wholistic understanding of man can be presented in the funeral which regards the body of the deceased as one of its legitimate focuses. The memorial service by its very combination of function and form makes such a unitary understanding of man more difficult.

The potential danger of the memorial service is that it conveys meanings which are essentially dualistic, ascetic, and docetic. All three of these classical points of view hold that the spirit is separable from the material, that spirit is good and matter is evil, and that spirit is real and permanent while the material is transient and unreal. The memorial service is prevented from presenting a wholistic understanding of man because a portion of man is consciously and deliberately excluded from its form. Although it must be admitted that through misunderstanding the funeral too can miss the meaning of man as totality, the funeral does offer a potential for affirming man as a unity because no portion of his being is deliberately excluded. The funeral is not committed by its very nature to a dualistic approach while the memorial service cannot easily avoid such a stance.

A second potential risk arises from the effort of the memorial service to reduce, or even to eliminate, the expression of emotion. We have already indicated that the sanction-

213

ing of the release of feelings is a part of the valuable function of the funeral properly conceived. Both the funeral and the memorial service have as a purpose the lessening of emotional strain, but each seeks to accomplish this goal in a different way. Here we have an illustration of the difference of the mechanisms of sublimation and repression. The funeral can channel emotion into patterns of release that are most helpful by symbolizing shared loss, by encouraging recollection of the deceased, by presenting realistically the separation which death brings. The memorial service often has as one of its purposes the avoidance of stimulating emotional expressions. In this sense it can tend toward the repression of feelings. The funeral can aid in the assimilation of the mourners' feelings, helping them to experience their feelings authentically; while the memorial service appears to encourage dissociation from the feelings that accompany loss.

The hasty disposal of the body may well be for some a means for evading the therapeutic pain of facing the reality of death by visual encounter with the body of the deceased. They feel that it is easier to avoid painful recollection without the focal point of the body which has so long been the point of contact in relationships with the deceased.

If the memorial service is scheduled too long after the death occurs, it brings community support to the mourners in the later stages of their bereavement. Consequently this support can be less meaningful and helpful because the mourners have been left to face the major traumas devoid of such sustaining. To delay the funeral for too many days following death would have essentially the same effect.

The memorial service, symbolized by the early disposition of the body, tends to put bereavement on an intellectual basis. The reduction of visual stimuli, the lack of any sense of tangible presence of even a part of what has been known as the deceased person, immediately establishes a context which tends to put everything into the realm of thinking rather than

214

feeling. The fact that this arrangement is conscious and deliberate makes the intention of avoiding certain emotionally stimulating factors readily apparent. The memorial service does not necessarily have to substitute intellectualization for emotional expression. The service could be planned to take this dimension into account. But the structure too often implies the purpose of avoidance, making it very difficult to escape repression.

The effort of the memorial service to focus totally on life contrasts with the possibility of focusing on the conjunction of life and death in the funeral. One of the fairly representative statements of principle of groups supporting memorial services affirms: "We wish our memory image of the departed to be centered on a life in its fullness and not on a corpse. . . . It is common for those of us who feel as we do to have a memorial service or meeting in a private home or church or other meaningful place some days after death, and entirely apart from the body. The emphasis at this meeting is placed on the living qualities of the person, rather than on death." [3] Such intentions, which may well be reactions against earlier excesses which turned the funeral into overemphasis on death, constitute an overreaction to the other extreme. Seen against the pattern of vitalism so apparent in our culture, this can easily become a part of the avoidance and escape formula that directs contemporary attitudes.

The concerted effort of the memorial service to orient itself toward life, while at the same time consciously avoiding symbols of the reality of death, sustains the efforts of our generation to separate death from life. It becomes a studied denial of the fact that death is truly a part of life, that the two realities are dynamically related.

Although it is possible for the funeral to be excessively morbid, to focus too intently upon death, this is not a neces-

[3] *Manual of Simple Burial* (2nd ed.; Burnsville, N. C.: The Celo Press, 1964), p. 13.

215

sary emphasis. The funeral has the potential capacity for considering life and death in conjunction. The memorial service, however, does not have a similar potentiality because there is built into its function and form unavoidable elements of denial and diversion.

The survey reported by Fulton [4] finds that in a comparison of members of memorial societies and a random nationwide population sample there was considerably less attendance of funerals by the memorial group than by the general population group. Fulton states:

However, rational thought and scientific skepticism are confounded by death, so we found this same group [the memorial group] was most anxious of the three groups to avoid or disguise its [death's] presence or possibility. This is demonstrated by such findings as their desire to eliminate the body from the funeral, their greater avoidance of funerals and their greater reluctance to permit their children to attend a funeral ceremony. It is worthy of note that such a finding as the latter is inconsistent with all that characterizes the style of child rearing of such professional and progressive groups as this. Typically families of the social, professional, and intellectual level of the members of the memorial group strove to bring their children up in a world of reality through the discouraging of such fantasies as ghosts, hobgoblins, Santa Claus, and the bogies of sex. Nevertheless, in this setting they appear to behave contrary to form and seek to shield the ultimate truth from their children.[5]

It certainly should not be assumed that every person who prefers a memorial service to a funeral is seeking to evade the reality of death. There are some who have reflected sufficiently upon death to have come to terms with its reality. They do not necessarily require the kinds of reinforcement and support which the funeral provides. A memorial service may be quite

[4] Robert L. Fulton, *The Sacred and the Secular.*
[5] *Ibid.,* p. 11.

appropriate to their needs. But it must be observed that this is not always the case and that a memorial service planned as a conscious or unconscious evasion of the reality of death and some of the pain of working through grief will not fulfill for the individual the same helpful function that a funeral might. The memorial service pattern is just as susceptible as the funeral, if not more so, to warping by those elements of the American view of life and death which call for avoidance, control, and the radical separation of the reality of death from the reality of life.

It must be admitted that the convenience and economy of the memorial service offer some practical advantages over the funeral. The memorial service makes possible wider participation because of the convenient time at which it can be scheduled, usually in the evening hours. The emphasis on simplicity that characterizes many memorial services enables an economy that is in many instances desirable. However, it should not necessarily be assumed that the funeral is inordinately more expensive. Either service could be the occasion for unjustifiable extravagance. It might also be asserted that the presence of the body of the deceased at the funeral necessitates additional expense for preparation. The question really is: Is such added expense justifiable? Does it enable a valid benefit? Or to put it another way, if it can be demonstrated that the presence of the body is helpful to the bereaved on psychological, social, and theological grounds, is some reasonable additional expense warranted?

Our reaction to the memorial service is that it has both liabilities and values which influence our proposal for new designs for the funeral. The close correlation of the form of the memorial service with its stated functions (even though one may not entirely agree with the value of those functions) is an admirable model for the funeral. Perhaps it is due to the fact that the memorial service is a relatively young custom compared to the long tradition which in part guides funeral

217

custom. But more than this, it is probably due to the fact that those who plan memorial services are guided by reasonably clear ideas of what they want and are exercising their freedom to get it. The new designs for the funeral need similar thoughtful understanding of the functions which the funeral should fulfill. So while we would disagree with a number of the major functions of the memorial service and the forms which follow, the thoughtful, deliberate, and reasoned approach of its planners is admirable. It is our hope that studies such as this one will produce an equally thoughtful approach to the funeral.

The new designs for the funeral would contradict such functions of the memorial service as the effort to avoid any attention to the body of the deceased, to detour the expression of feelings by removing as many emotional stimuli as possible, and to lay the single major emphasis on life rather than on the conjunction of life and death. These endeavors are evaluated as potentially productive of inhibitions in the mourning process, circumvention of a number of the valuable resources that have been demonstrated to be helpful to the bereaved, and misunderstanding of the relation of life and death and of the nature of man. Observation of these dangers in the memorial service help to make the new designs for the funeral more meaningful.

Similarly, we can learn from the values of the memorial service—convenience, simplicity, and economy. The importance of enabling as many persons as possible to participate in the funeral has already been indicated. The flexibility of the time schedule of the memorial service gives us guidance at this point. It also indicates that convenience in time schedule is restricted largely by the necessity for disposition of the body after the funeral. So it is seen that restoring the funeral to its original form as an expression of group solidarity hinges upon a reasonable solution to the problem of when and how disposition of the body shall be made.

The memorial service indicates clearly the necessity for considering simplicity and economy in the light of the values gained or lost. Neither simplicity nor economy can be ends in themselves, quite apart from what is accomplished or neglected through them. While both are appropriate considerations in the new designs for the funeral, they must always be weighed fully in keeping with the values being sought in a particular funeral. Extravagance is always open to serious question, but different mourners have varying needs which may require different scales of expenses. The cost of preparation of a body after an accident, for example, may be entirely justifiable for mourners who need confirmation of the reality of their loss. Even the expense of a costlier coffin than is actually necessary may be in some exceptional instances reasonable as a means of seeking to make restitution to one who has been wronged. Certainly this should not be misinterpreted as an endorsement for the excesses to which one can all too often point, but at the same time appreciation of deeper needs present in some mourners can also indicate the dangers of costly economy.

Thus, although we would not find merit in some of the goals of the memorial service, we recognize that any study of the funeral can learn a good deal from this contemporary custom.

Privatization of the Funeral

There is a recurrent strain in these various modern mortuary practices. Customs such as the participation in the viewing rather than the funeral service and private committal rites followed later by a memorial service point to a tendency toward the privatization of bereavement and the resources for meeting it.

Of course, it cannot be denied that mourning is intensely personal. But it also has its corporate dimension which ultimately brings important resources to the mourner. This fact needs to be acknowledged. Too often there is concern about sparing the bereaved the embarrassment of showing their feelings before a group of friends and neighbors. Why should this be an embarrassment in a concerned and accepting community? Yet funerals are criticized for putting mourners on display, or arrangements are made to have the major mourners totally cut off from the assembled group by putting them in an isolated "family room" at the mortuary.

Or we find statements such as that made by Harmer: "By restricting attendance at the funeral, the persons closest to the dead would be freed from the obligation of putting on a show to impress casual on-lookers." [6] Even if we grant that in the funeral at times social expectations cause the mourners to respond with inauthentic feeling, we cannot imply that all emotional expressions by the mourners are not genuine. Nor should we hold that the funeral should be privatized to enable real feelings to be expressed. If individuals are so alienated from each other in our society that they have no basis for sharing genuine feeling, will people be helped by deepening their isolation? A far more adequate solution would seem to be to educate people to the value of the expression of the feelings and to the important function of the funeral as a group sanctioning of that release.

The funeral is not a public display but a group sharing the deep sorrows of some of its number. The difficulty manifested through the growing number of evasive mechanisms in mourning says more about the condition of our depersonalized social structure than it does of the adequacy of the funeral. The fragmentation of relationships and the interpersonal distance which we have noted in our urbanizing culture are truly regrettable. Every means should be taken to improve the situation by emphasizing that the needs of mourners are much the same in rural or urban, agrarian or industrial societies and

[6] Ruth M. Harmer, *The High Cost of Dying*, p. 227-28.

that the resources for meeting these needs are produced in relationship. One way in which this can be done is to restore the public context of the funeral and to resist its privatization.

It can be argued that the unacceptability of public expressions of sorrow and all the related feelings that are possible tends to encourage many of the aberrations for which the funeral has been condemned. For example, the desire to find social status through a lavish funeral can be seen as an acceptable way of expressing a sense of loss which the mourner feels but cannot express because such emotion would be regarded cynically as display or weakness. The mourner's tears are socially unacceptable, so he releases his feelings with his checkbook.

If the funeral were properly restored in its public—that is, its group—dimension, it would truly serve the needs of the bereaved more effectively. Thus new designs for the funeral need to reverse the slow trend toward privatization by taking a number of steps.

The funeral should develop a form that enables the widest possible radius of social participation by making it convenient for persons who share the loss with the immediate family of the deceased to participate.

A deepening sense of group involvement in death and bereavement should be supported. Those who attend the funeral should not merely observe but should actually participate in the rites, making the funeral a genuine group experience.

The funeral needs to lay constant emphasis on the nature of the group in terms not of contiguity but of acceptance. The mere gathering of a group of people is not enough. This group must be supportive by manifesting empathetic understanding of the bereaved and by accepting them with all of their feelings.

Thus restoration of the funeral to its social context is a vital part of the new designs.

Freedom in the Funeral

The final issue with which we would deal is the issue of freedom. Most studies of the funeral, both the sympathetic and the critical, the serious and the satirical, have pointed up rightly the need for greater freedom. The funeral fulfills its functions far less adequately when the mourners are not acting on the basis of their own wishes and feelings. Helpfulness is reduced when they are merely responding to the pressures of others or just conforming to patterns which lack meaning for them.

Individuals should have freedom of choice in setting patterns for the funerals of their loved ones. But these choices must be based upon solid foundations. Persons should be educated to the fact that there are a number of standards by which their choices are made. There should be awareness of the psychological factors in mourning and the way in which the funeral seeks to meet the emotional needs of the bereaved. Particular emphasis must be placed upon the dangers created by evasion and escapism.

There should be a basic theological orientation for the religious person or a philosophical orientation for the humanist which relates his individual experience to the larger meanings of life and death. There should be knowledge of the social dimensions of bereavement so that the benefits of the support and acceptance of a participating group are understood.

There should be appreciation for the economic factors in the funeral so that a sensible distinction can be made between those elements which are benefits worth paying for and those which are unnecessarily expensive because they truly serve no helpful function or seek to provide values which could be secured in much less costly ways.

Freedom is enhanced in direct proportion to the number of alternatives which exist. Free choice is more truly present when an individual has thought through all of the potentialities of the funeral in the light of a reasonably correct understanding of its functions.

New designs for the funeral would offer the possibility of wider and more meaningful choice. However, this would not be a chaotic or unstructured choice. There would be acknowledgment of the values which are to be found in the funeral and pointed criticism of the excesses, deviations, and failures present in contemporary funeral patterns. Because the new designs proposed here are founded upon awareness of elements in the feelings and experiences of the mourners, free choice of the kind of service is more likely than it would be with thoughtless and indifferent random planning or with mere conformity to custom.

One of the important features of the new designs we are proposing here is that a direction is suggested rather than specific content decreed. The particular elements of content need to be worked out on an individual and local basis. Certainly more than one possible variation of the forms of the funeral can be worked out. We have already suggested one such major variation in the delineation of the religious and humanistic funerals. Individual needs and local situations will commend other modifications.

It should be remembered, however, that the functions of the funeral do not change. Individual instances do not bring a completely new set of functions into play. Rather there is a kind of selectivity or ranking of the functions of the funeral which constitutes the area in which the individual choices are made. Even more individual adaptation is possible in setting the forms which the funeral should take, so long as they remain consistent with its functions.

Conclusion

It would be folly to propose that the contemporary funeral is fully adequate and that the status quo should be preserved.

It is equally incorrect to assert that the funeral is totally without value and should be discarded as an empty vestige.

Our proposals for new designs for the funeral are based upon a desire to conserve the values of the functions of the funeral indicated by an interdisciplinary study of the needs of the bereaved. These values are supported by research and reflection in theology and in the behavioral sciences.

Present inadequacies in the funeral are largely due to the fact that the functions of the funeral as we have described them have been ignored or circumvented by some of the forms of the funeral. Poor design has resulted because form has not followed function properly. Our proposals seek to remedy this discrepancy.

Our proposals for new designs are not intended to be complete innovations because it is our conviction that the funeral has much value in it which can be conserved. New forms need to be developed constantly in accordance with individual needs and local situations, but they need to come into being in accordance with a broad understanding of and firm commitment to the functions which enable the funeral to serve the needs of the mourners. Only in this way will the funeral be seen as an experience of value rather than as a useless vestige.

Appendix

Guide for Group Discussion
of the Funeral

Because, as we have seen, the funeral is both personal and social in nature, it is not enough that an individual reflect upon the kind of funeral he would like for himself or a member of his family. It is also valuable for groups which are involved in the lives of individuals to express a general consensus regarding the functions and forms which they feel to be beneficial to all when death disrupts the group.

With new interest in the funeral in recent years, a few churches and a variety of memorial societies have framed normative statements about what funerals ought to be and do. Some of these formulations have been thoughtful and comprehensive; others have limited themselves to more or less peripheral matters.

Most of those who are concerned for the status of the funeral in our culture have recognized that the effectiveness of the funeral, however they define it, will be enhanced by broad public education. Congressional investigations may be able to produce effective regulation of some of the economic aspects of the funeral. Satires may be able to stir public interest in some of the problems involved in contemporary practices. Memorial societies may focalize the efforts of their memberships to develop patterns that suit their preference. But only widespread, thoughtful, comprehensive discussion of the nature and purpose of the funeral offers promise of making it an effective aid for those who suffer bereavement.

In order to encourage such discussion in churches, in memorial societies, in community groups, this guide is proposed. If the amount of time that a group can give to the discussion is limited, rather than omitting portions of the outline, it is suggested that individuals be designated to prepare for presentation sections I and III, using section II as the major arena for group participation. It is to be hoped, however, that any group seeking to fulfill a useful purpose through such discussion will give sufficient time and preparation to permit approach to the subject in some depth.

I. Evaluating the Funeral

Thoughtful consideration of the funeral is the only way in which it can be decided whether the funeral is vestige or value. On the basis of that decision either support is withdrawn from this ceremony as a meaningful way of helping the bereaved or serious and creative thought is given to ways in which the funeral can be made fully adequate for meeting the needs of mourners.

Many evaluations of the funeral have been made. Funeral interests have valued it highly as a ceremonial accompaniment of death designed to bring honor to the memory of the deceased and a measure of support and comfort to the bereaved. Critics of the funeral have devalued it as irrelevant, anachronistic, extravagant, pagan. The church has been ambivalent— on the one hand valuing the funeral as one of the traditional rites of the church to mark the ending of a life and to sustain the mourners; on the other hand seeing the funeral as overly materialistic or superficially sentimental. Students of the funeral in the fields of anthropology, psychology, and pastoral theology value it as a useful means by which both individual and group fulfill the various needs brought into focus by the crisis of death.

Each individual has both the right and the responsibility to

226

assess for himself the value of the funeral. On what basis will he make his evaluation? The position developed by this study is that many norms are required for a proper evaluation of the funeral. It is not enough just to look at the mortician's bill or at the customs that have been accepted by default. Every available norm should be brought into play to provide a balanced picture of what is helpful and what is not helpful in the funeral.

Ten norms are presented here for your consideration. They are based upon the findings of behavioral science and pastoral theology. Detailed explanation of these norms will be found in chapter 5.

As these norms are discussed, the focus of attention should be their validity and their value. The ways in which these normative understandings of the funeral are implemented will be dealt with in the following section.

For each of the norms these questions might be posed: What does this norm mean to you? Why do you regard this function of the funeral helpful or not helpful to the bereaved? In what ways, if any, would this norm change with the times or with social patterns? On what basis would you regard this a valid, or invalid, norm for evaluating the funeral?

1. An adequate funeral should provide an opportunity for the manifestation of a shared loss and a means by which the support of the community of mourners is conveyed to the bereaved.
2. The funeral should express social understanding of the relationship of the living to those who have died.
3. The funeral should begin the process of strengthening relational patterns among the living.
4. The funeral should assist in the reinforcement of reality for the bereaved.
5. The funeral should aid the necessary recollection of the deceased and the beginning of the recapitulation of relationship.

6. The funeral, by conveying an element of finality in death, should eventuate in the freedom for developing new relational patterns without violation of the integrity of previous relationship with the deceased.
7. The funeral should offer an opportunity for the release of feelings of the mourners.
8. The funeral should enable mourners to be more meaningfully related to religious (or philosophical) resources for understanding and accepting suffering.
9. The funeral should, at least in rudimentary form, develop a perspective on the meanings of life and death in the light of the crisis of death.
10. The funeral should assist the mourners intellectually and emotionally to comprehend more fully the nature of man (for the Christian; as a body-spirit totality; for the humanist; as a body-mind unity).

II. Putting the Norms to Use

Here we would make an effort to consider as many as possible of the components of funerals in your community. It may be that this task will have to be divided among members of the discussion group or among subgroups and then reported to the whole group.

List as many as possible of the elements of funeral practice in the common experience of the group. You may find things to be added to this suggested list.

embalming
cosmetic preparation of the
  body
wooden casket
bronze casket
burial vault
viewing at the mortuary

floral tributes
memorial gifts
friends bring food to home
  of mourners
open casket at the funeral
closed casket at funeral
pall

public funeral service

private funeral service

funeral at the church

quiet music before the funeral

solo or small choir

hymn by the congregation (or unison reading of a poem)

scripture readings (or readings from works of a great thinker)

group joining in a statement of its faith

factual obituary

eulogy

prayers

funeral sermon or address

Lord's Prayer in unison

procession to cemetery or crematory

limousines for family of deceased

police escort to cemetery

artificial grass at grave site

flowers at the grave

committal service

cremation immediately following death

memorial service in lieu of funeral

entombment in mausoleum

notices of death in newspapers

rituals of fraternal or veteran groups

Some of the questions which might then be asked are: According to the norms that have been discussed, how do you evaluate each of these funeral practices? Are there any of these customs or practices which you feel are not justified by the norms you apply? What revisions in forms or new forms seem necessary in order to fulfill the normative functions of the funeral?

What responsibility does your group have for assisting individual members in planning funerals that will be of maximum help to them in bereavement? What are the advantages of general structures of the funeral agreed upon in common by the group? What is the responsibility of the group when a member makes decisions that are contradicted by the norms acceptable to the group?

III. Evaluating Innovations

There is no need to regard the funeral as static. Although its functions may not be subject to a great deal of variation, there is considerable room for the development of new forms.

One of the major proposals of this volume is the need for distinction between the religious funeral and the humanistic funeral. This is an effort to enable the funeral to convey meanings relevant to the mourners' orientation. What advantages do you see in such a proposal? What risks are involved? What steps do you think can be taken to make the religious funeral more meaningful? How should proposals for the humanistic funeral be implemented? On what basis should it be decided whether a religious or a humanistic funeral should be planned?

Another proposal made here is that funerals be scheduled at times when wider social participation is possible. What would be the possibilities for such innovation in your community? What are some of the difficulties that might be encountered in such an arrangement? What solutions could you offer to make possible maximum group support through the funeral?

Too long have people assumed either that the funeral was such a sensitive subject that it should not be dealt with in objective, critical discussion, or that the funeral was so immutable or inviolable that constructive discussion would be purposeless. Neither of these assumptions is valid. It is to be hoped that open and sensible consideration of the funeral, beginning with some questions such as those outlined in this discussion guide, will direct persons and groups in the planning of more helpful and meaningful funerals.

BIBLIOGRAPHY

Books

Allport, Gordon. *Pattern and Growth in Personality.* New York: Holt, Rinehart & Winston, 1961.

Bachmann, C. Charles. *Ministering to the Grief Sufferer.* Englewood Cliffs: Prentice-Hall, 1964.

Bendann, Effie. *Death Customs: An Analytical Study of Burial Rites.* New York: Alfred A. Knopf, 1930.

Benedict, Ruth. *Patterns of Culture.* New York: The New American Library, 1959.

Bonhoeffer, Dietrich. *Ethics.* Ed. Eberhard, Bethge, trans. by Neville Smith. New York: The Macmillan Company, 1955.

Bossard, James, and Boll, Eleanor. *Ritual in Family Living.* Philadelphia: University of Pennsylvania Press, 1950.

Bowers, Margaretta, et al. *Counseling the Dying.* New York: Thomas Nelson and Sons, 1964.

Bowman, LeRoy. *The American Funeral: A Study in Guilt, Extravagance and Sublimity.* Washington, D.C.: Public Affairs Press, 1959.

Bultmann, Rudolf. "New Testament and Mythology," *Kerygma and Myth,* Vol. I. Ed. Hans W. Bartsch, trans. by Reginald Fuller. London: S.P.C.K. Press, 1953.

Choron, Jacques. *Death and Western Thought.* New York: Collier Books, 1963.

———. *Modern Man and Mortality.* New York: The Macmillan Company, 1964.

Covey, Cyclone. *The American Pilgrimage*. New York: Collier Books, 1961.

Cullmann, Oscar. *The Early Church*. Ed. A. J. B. Higgins, trans. by A. J. B. Higgins and S. Godman. Philadelphia: Westminster Press, 1956.

———. *Immortality of the Soul or Resurrection of the Dead?* London: Epworth Press, 1958.

Dahl, M. E. *The Resurrection of the Body*. Naperville: Alec R. Allenson, 1962.

Davis, George W. *Existentialism and Theology*. New York: Philosophical Library, 1957.

Eissler, K. R. *The Psychiatrist and the Dying Patient*. New York: International Universities Press, 1955.

Eliade, Mircea. *Birth and Rebirth*. Trans. by Willard R. Trask. New York: Harper & Brothers, 1958.

———. *Patterns in Comparative Religion*. Trans. by Rosemary Sheed. New York: Sheed and Ward, 1958.

Farberow, Norman L. (ed.). *Taboo Topics*. New York: Atherton Press, 1964.

Farberow, Norman L., and Shneidman, Edwin S. (eds.). *The Cry for Help*. New York: McGraw-Hill Company, 1961.

Feifel, Herman. "Death—Relevant Variable in Psychology," *Existential Psychology*. Ed. Rollo May. New York: Random House, 1961.

———. "Death," *Taboo Topics*. Ed. Norman L. Farberow. New York: Atherton Press, 1964.

———. (ed.). *The Meaning of Death*. New York: McGraw-Hill Book Company, 1959.

Frazer, J. G. *The Belief in Immortality and the Worship of the Dead*. 3 vols. London: Macmillan and Company, 1913-1922.

Freud, Sigmund. *Collected Papers*, Vol. IV. New York: Basic Books, 1959.

Fulton, Robert L. (ed.). *Death and Identity*. New York: John Wiley & Sons, 1965.

———. *The Sacred and the Secular: Attitudes of the American Public Toward Death*. Milwaukee: Bulfin Printers, 1963.

Goppelt, Leonhard, et al. The Easter Message Today. Trans. by Salvator Attanasio, and Darrell Guder. New York: Thomas Nelson and Sons, 1964.

Habenstein, Robert W., and Lamers, William M. Funeral Customs the World Over. Milwaukee: Bulfin Printers, 1960.

———. The History of American Funeral Directing. Milwaukee: Bulfin Printers, 1962.

Harmer, Ruth Mulvey. The High Cost of Dying. New York: Collier Books, 1963.

Henry, Jules. Culture Against Man. New York: Random House, 1963.

Hocking, William E. Thoughts on Death and Life. New York: Harper & Brothers, 1937.

Irion, Paul E. The Funeral and the Mourners. Nashville: Abingdon Press, 1954.

Jackson, Edgar N. For the Living. Des Moines: Channel Press, 1964.

———. Understanding Grief. Nashville: Abingdon Press, 1957.

James, E. O. Prehistoric Religion. London: Thames and Hudson, 1957.

Lamont, Corliss. A Humanist Funeral Service. New York: Horizon Press, 1954.

Lerner, Max. America as a Civilization. New York: Simon and Schuster, 1957.

Lewis, C. S., A Grief Observed. Greenwich, Conn.: Seabury Press, 1961.

Malinowski, Bronislaw. "The Art of Magic and the Power of Faith," Theories of Society, Vol. II. Ed. Talcott Parsons, New York: Free Press, 1961.

———. Magic, Science, and Religion and Other Essays. Boston: Beacon Press, 1948.

Manual of Simple Burial. 2nd ed. Burnsville, N. C.: The Celo Press, 1964.

Marcuse, Herbert. Eros and Civilization. New York: Vintage Books, 1962.

Mead, Margaret. "The Immortality of Man," The Nature of Man. Ed. Simon Doniger. New York: Harper & Row, 1962.

233

Miller, Samuel. *The Dilemma of Modern Belief.* New York: Harper & Row, 1963.

Mitford, Jessica. *The American Way of Death.* New York: Simon and Schuster, 1963.

Myers, F. W. *Human Personality and Its Survival of Bodily Death.* New York: Longmans, Green and Company, 1903.

Owen, D. R. G. *Body and Soul.* Philadelphia: Westminster Press, 1956.

Parrinder, Geoffrey. *Worship in the World's Religions.* London: Faber and Faber, 1961.

Pelikan, Jaroslav. *The Shape of Death.* Nashville: Abingdon Press, 1961.

Puckle, Bertram S. *Funeral Customs.* New York: Frederick A. Stokes Company, 1926.

Radin, Paul. *Primitive Man as Philosopher.* New York: Dover Publications, 1958.

Rahner, Karl. *On the Theology of Death.* Trans. by Charles H. Henkey. New York: Herder & Herder, 1961.

Richardson, Alan. *An Introduction to the Theology of the New Testament.* New York: Harper & Row, 1958.

Robinson, John A. T. *The Body.* London: SCM Press, 1952.

Rogers, William F. *Ye Shall be Comforted.* Philadelphia: Westminster Press, 1950.

Scherzer, Carl J. *Ministering to the Dying.* Englewood Cliffs: Prentice-Hall, 1963.

Shneidman, Edwin S. "Suicide," *Taboo Topics.* Ed. Norman L. Farberow. New York: Atherton Press, 1964.

Sulzberger, Cyrus L. *My Brother Death.* New York: Harper & Brothers, 1961.

van Gennep, Arnold. *The Rites of Passage.* Trans. by Monika Vizedom, and Gabrielle Caffee. Chicago: University of Chicago Press, 1960.

Warner, W. Lloyd. *The Living and the Dead.* New Haven: Yale University Press, 1959.

Articles

Borkenau, Franz. "The Concept of Death," *The Twentieth Century*, 1955, pp. 313-29.

Dahl, Edward C. "A Funeral Ministry to the Unchurched," *Pulpit Digest*, XXXII (1952), 11-16.

"Death: A Special Issue," a symposium in *motive* (January-February 1964).

Fulton, Robert L. "The Clergyman and the Funeral Director: A Study in Role Conflict," *Social Forces*, XXXVII (1961), 317-23.

————. "Death and the Self," *Journal of Religion and Health*, III (1964), 359-68.

Harbison, Janet. "New Patterns for American Funerals," *Presbyterian Life* (August 1, 1964), pp. 8 ff.

Lindemann, Erich. "Symptomatology and Management of Acute Grief," *The American Journal of Psychiatry*, CI (1944), 141-49.

Matz, Milton. "Judaism and Bereavement," *Journal of Religion and Health*, III (1964), 345-52.

Oglesby, William B. "The Resurrection and the Funeral," *Pastoral Psychology* (November 1957), pp. 11-16.

INDEX

Date Due

BROADMAN
B P
SUPPLIES

Code 4386-04, CLS-4, Broadman Supplies, Nashville, Tenn., Printed in U.S.A.